AUTHOR'S PI

The conclusions set forth in this l
than twenty years of study and research in my efforts to find a
unifying theme common to all development systems that
promise personal growth, mind expansion and spiritual enlightenment. In my research in psychology and psychiatry, I
became aware of the wide application of hypnosis as a
therapeutic tool. I determined I would study the science of
hypnotism in a comprehensive way under the best teacher I
could discover. Much of the material in this book, theoretical
as well as practical, was stimulated by the remarkable teachings and influence of an extraordinary man, Gil Boyne, who
operates the Hypnotism Training Institute of Los Angeles in
Glendale, California, a suburb of Los Angeles, where he
teaches "Hypnotism as a Career."

I first met Gil Boyne in 1970, when I enrolled in his class in
self hypnosis. I had interviewed or investigated a number of
other hypnotists and hypnotherapists. None of them impressed
me, and I was about to give up the idea when I spoke with a
psychiatrist who was a neighbor of mine. When the subject of
hypnotism arose, he told me he had been greatly impressed by
a hypnotist who had given a series of lecture-demonstrations to
the Neuropsychiatric Department at U.C.L.A. My visit to this
man was the beginning of an experience that changed my life,
as well as the life of my wife Joyce.

We were quickly captivated by our own imaginations, as we
became aware of the fantastic potential of self hypnosis as a
primary method for redirecting our own energies into more
creative living. We were even more captivated by the charisma
and personal power and magnetism of Gil Boyne. I always had
the sense of watching a gifted artist at work when I watched
him induce a hypnotic trance in a matter of seconds. I have
never seen anyone induce hypnosis as fast as Gil Boyne does.
By the end of the course we both could hypnotize ourselves and
program our deeper minds in a matter of minutes.

We continued our studies with Gil Boyne in Professional
Hypnosis and Advanced Hypnotherapy. I hope to communi-

cate to you, the reader, some of the unusual and amazing experiences that were part of my training.

Mr. Boyne calls his method of overcoming the negative scripts of the past, "POWER PROGRAMMING"! He has revised the stereotyped concepts of Auto-suggestion and created the first totally new methods in more than forty years! He has a rare talent for distilling and integrating psychological and spiritual truths into a concise and practical philosophy that stimulates growth and movement in all who begin to use it. Gil Boyne is an intensely creative human being who delights in his participation in life. I believe it is these qualities of exuberance and intense dedication that enable him to stimulate and excite his students to raise their image of their own creative potential.

Gil Boyne teaches his methods to capacity classes five nights a week, and in the many classes I attended I met an extraordinary cross-section of humanity, ranging from aspiring performers to celebrated super-stars and athletes, from bank tellers to corporation presidents. Some of the people I met at Gil Boyne's Self-Help Institute are: comedienne Lily Tomlin; National Bowling Champion Barry Asher; Sylvester Stallone, writer and star of the film "Rocky"; the charismatic TV minister, Reverend Ike; Lloyd Haines, TV star of "Room 222"; Lisa Todd of TV's "Hee Haw"; film and TV star Sheree North; famed concert violinist Endre Balogh; writer Jane Wagner (writer-producer for Lily Tomlin); Elleson Trevor ("Flight of the Phoenix"); and Ray Parker, writer for Art Linkletter, Bob Hope and Dick Van Dyke. In short, all kinds of people from all walks of life come to study with the man whom I consider to be the world's foremost authority on subconscious motivation through hypnosis, the man whose methods I will describe in this book.

I have listened to many people report rapid and dramatic changes in their lives, but for me, the most impressive case was my own. About a year ago I awoke one morning and found myself partially paralyzed. I had suffered a severe stroke during the night, and was unable to speak or make myself understood except by crude scribbling. The doctors in the Santa Monica Hospital ran a series of tests, and informed my wife I could expect partial recovery in about six months. It was then I applied Gil Boyne's principles of subconscious programming through self hypnosis! I set my goal of complete communication with others for one week, and hypnotized myself right there in the emergency room of the hospital. In three days I was discharged from the hospital with my doctor reporting ninety percent recovery. The right side of my face, which had sagged noticeably, was completely normal, and I was able to write again with ease! I recovered completely within a week or so, and presently I am in the best of health.

Much of the inspiration for this book and the energy to begin writing it was the result of my studies with Gil Boyne, and I have come to regard him as a close personal friend. It is with great admiration and deep affection that I dedicate this book to the man who made it possible, Mr. Gil Boyne.

Postscript, March, 1985

For more than seven years, I studied with and worked for Gil Boyne and often saw him create "Miracles On Demand!" Because of his incredible commitment to maximum results in minimum time, I consider him to be the most effective hypnotherapist in the world today. My training with Gil Boyne has transformed my career and my personal life as well. I proudly acknowledge him as my "mentor."

Since this book was published in 1977 it has become the bestselling book on Self-Hypnosis in America. In addition, it has brought me recognition and status as an author and hypnotherapist. In 1979, I established the Hypnotism Training Institute of Washington, which is now the largest and most successful Training Institute in the Pacific Northwest.

I receive great satisfaction in training hypnotherapists in the Gil Boyne system because of his total commitment to helping hypnotherapists maximize their effectiveness and his rare talent for creative teaching and his outstanding therapeutic innovations.

Charles Tebbetts, Director
Hypnotism Training Institute Of Washington
Lynnwood, Washington

I receive great satisfaction in training hypnotherapists in the Gil Boyne system because of his total commitment to helping hypnotherapists maximize their effectiveness and his rare talent for creative teaching and his outstanding therapeutic innovations.

Charles Tebetts, Director
Hypnotism Training Institute Of Washington
Lynnwood, Washington

CONTENTS

INTRODUCTION

Thousands of pages have been written advising us to cast off our negative attitudes and think positively. We read the words, agree with the principles, but continue to act as our old established habits dictate. The conscious mind agrees but the subconscious does not, creating a stalemate.

The goal of this book will be to not only convince you of the desirability of behavior modification, but to show you how to modify it. It is not enough to convince your conscious, reasoning mind that some of your habits should be changed. Only as you learn to re-program your subconscious mind will you be free to act according to your conscious desires.

Of course, there are many cases in which our conscious mind also needs to be corrected. We will not initiate action to reprogram the subconscious unless we believe the reprogramming will be beneficial. A woman may feel her hatred of all men is justified because of limited unpleasant experiences with a few of them. A man who was taught as a child that it was admirable to be the bully of the neighborhood may feel proud of his over-aggressive behavior. This book will list each harmful emotion, convince the conscious, reasoning mind of its destructive nature, and then explain how to influence the subconscious mind to agree. This will enable the reader to coordinate the two parts of the mind so they will work harmoniously to modify destructive, self-defeating behavior patterns.

Some teachers of "Mind Control Systems" reject the term "Hypnosis," yet they induce a trance state by inhibiting the awareness of the conscious mind, or as many of them call it, the "outer awareness," and heighten the awareness of the subconscious, or as they call it, the creative intelligence. By any definition, this is the trance state of self-hypnosis, although the denials may be loud. There is still a difference in the total process, in that meditation students go into the trance expecting only the general set of results they have been indoctrinated to believe probable, while in self-hypnosis they choose their own suggestions and accelerate specific desired changes.

This book will also show meditators how to take advantage of their already learned trance induction by adding the dynamic power of auto-suggestion for faster and more gratifying results.

It will give you a condensed explanation, including the how-to, of hypnosis, self-hypnosis, TM, fractional relaxation, bio-feedback, auto-suggestion, faith healing, age regression, and ESP, all in one book.

Anyone willing to spend fifteen minutes twice daily for a few weeks practicing self-hypnosis induced by any method they choose and calling it by any name they choose can surely expand the power of their inner mind and enjoy a fuller and more expressive life. And those who go further and use auto-suggestion during their periods of mental relaxation can have practically anything in life they want.

It is difficult for the average intelligent individual to believe a simple ritual can induce a trance-like state which will enable him to experience an entirely new and more satisfying awareness of himself. But self-hypnosis is being practiced in some form or another by hundreds of thousands who consider it one of the most important discoveries of their lives. Meditation students have paid millions of dollars for over seven hundred and seventy thousand TM courses alone, and business and civic leaders all over the world use it daily. There must be a reason, and I will make it easy for you to give the trance a chance!

Find yourself and find
health, wealth and wisdom.

Chapter I

HOW TO FIND YOURSELF

Most people just muddle along day after day, realizing a small percentage of their potential, and hope luck or some other mysterious unknown force will eventually change their lives. They reach the age of disillusionment and look around them, wondering why they missed the boat. They don't realize it, but that unknown force is right there inside of them, waiting to be their obedient servant, and capable of giving them anything they want. A far-fetched idea? No. A scientifically proved fact. The secret starts with awareness expansion and is completed by auto-suggestion.

Awareness (or mind) expansion automatically stimulates a great deal of behavior modification by eliminating stress. Various forms of self-hypnosis, or meditation, when practiced over a period of several weeks bring about a noticeable decrease in anxiety and marked improvement in recall, academic performance and self-confidence, with bonus features

The Real YOU Has Dynamic Power You Seldom Use!

of psychological health and happiness. While in the self-imposed trance, auto-suggestion gives you the power to select the habits you wish to overcome or the weaknesses you wish to strengthen, and stimulates the subconscious to make your chosen corrections without conscious effort.

Expanded awareness is a new and often misunderstood term. You may believe you are as aware of your self, your feelings and your opinions as necessary, and this may be true. But you are only slightly aware of your subconscious or inner self.

THE TWO PARTS OF THE MIND

When you think of yourself you think of your conscious mind, the only mind you are fully aware of. It is your "me." It seems to make all your decisions and direct all your activity. But the largest and most dominant part of your mind is the part you are generally unaware of called the subconscious.

3

Your conscious mind may seem to call the shots but it is ruled by the desires of the subconscious, which is the real you. And until you learn to understand it, you do not know or understand yourself.

Many young people realize there is a void in their lives, and travel all over the world trying to "find" themselves. That elusive self can't be found by traveling, or even by looking behind the door or under the bed. The true self can be found by looking inward rather than outward.

Although we have free will to do anything we want to do, our decisions are based on the strength of our desires. And the subconscious desires always outweigh the conscious ones. A man may desire to remain in his warm bed on a cold winter morning instead of getting up and going to work. But if his subconscious mind has established a habit of wanting to get up to avoid losing his job, he will act seemingly against his will and get up, in spite of the unpleasant weather. An alcoholic may consciously desire to quit drinking. He regrets seeing his wife's love turning to disgust and his career going down the drain. Yet he will continue to drink to excess in spite of his conscious desire to quit. An obese person may consciously agree that he would be happier if he could control his eating habit and reduce his weight, yet he finds it impossible to do so. These people have accepted things consciously which they have been unable to accept in their inner or subconscious minds.

Although our conscious mind has the ability to reason and to decide upon the course of action that would be most advantageous to us, it cannot put its decision into action unless the subconscious agrees and directs its energy toward the implementation of our decisions. Our source of energy is the subconscious mind. No amount of will power exerted by the conscious mind can override it. It may allow the alcoholic to stay sober for one or two nights or the obese person to diet for a while, like an indulgent parent allowing a child a bit of leeway. But unless the subconscious is changed, the habits will continue to dominate, and will power can only dent the surface. Our subconscious acts the way it has been programmed to act, exactly as a computer does, and much of this programming occurred before we were old enough to discriminate between ideas helpful or detrimental to our welfare. For instance, if a young child is told by an irritated mother, "You never do anything right!" or "What's the matter with you? Can't you do anything?" this child will often be a failure as an adult. The critical factor in a child's conscious mind is not developed fully enough to censor this negative idea, so it becomes an established fact in his subconscious that he can't do things right. The subconscious has no critical factor, so it accepts as absolute truth any idea allowed to enter its computerlike system. The idea then becomes an integral part of the child's beliefs and consequent behavior. The conscious mind of an adult would reject the idea that he never does anything right and would not allow it to enter his subconscious.

The subconscious accepts only what the conscious mind believes at the time the suggestion is offered. But if the conscious mind changes an opinion after it has become entrenched in the subconscious, the subconscious will not change with it. The two parts of the mind will differ, and the subconscious opinion will be the dominant one. It will continue to dictate our desires and consequent behavior in spite of our conscious opinion.

The function of the conscious mind is to evaluate and compare each new idea it receives with previously accepted ideas and in this manner decide upon its veracity before accepting it in the subconscious memory bank. Remember, once the new idea is there, it becomes an absolute truth to the individual, and will be used to decide upon the acceptability of future ideas. Since many of the ideas accepted early in life are false, and many ideas accepted later are based upon the premise that the false ones are true, consider what a garbled assortment of half-truths, false fears and unreasonable hates and prejudices we accumulate during—and even after—our formative years!

Before the age of ten our uncritical minds are programmed by misinterpretations of chance events and the opinions and superstitions of those about us, who, in turn, were poorly programmed in their own formative years. It is obvious that we must change our subconscious minds if we are to achieve self-mastery. When this is accomplished, we can consciously direct our activity toward any goals we desire, including health, happiness, and financial success. If you change your mind you can live happily ever after!

HYPNOSIS AS A MEANS OF REACHING THE SUBCONSCIOUS

Since the subconscious mind is our driving force, we always do what our subconscious believes. Since it will believe anything it is told we can reprogram it if we bypass the conscious mind and substitute new, constructive ideas for its existing negative ones. Then they must be reinforced daily until they become well entrenched habits of thinking.

The following example will illustrate the futility of trying to reach the subconscious while the critical, conscious mind is aware. A bashful young man is invited to join the high school debating team because of his high academic rating. He agrees, and enjoys the honor, but is apprehensive because of his unreasoning fear of public speaking. He reasons in his conscious mind that there is no cause for his fear. Others much less articulate than he speak in public and so can he. But at this point his conscious mind gets a feedback from his subconscious where both his memory and his emotions reside and both are added to his reasoning. "Remember the last time you tried to speak before a crowd? Your voice trembled. Your hands shook so badly you couldn't read your notes. Your face turned red and you made a complete fool of yourself. It will happen again next time and you know it!" Fear and embarrassment accompany these thoughts, and his conscious mind cannot overcome his subconscious with all the logic he can muster. When the conscious and the subconscious are in conflict the subconscious usually wins, so his attempt at public speaking will be a failure.

This reasoning process with its subconscious conflicts must be temporarily suspended if the young man's subconscious is to be convinced it holds a false idea about his ability to speak in public. His subconscious is obviously wrong, because anyone can speak in public without embarrassment unless their subconscious believes differently.

We always do what our subconscious believes, even though we consciously know it is absurd. So the conscious mind must be put aside temporarily so our reasoning from a false premise can be halted, thus permitting us to substitute a correct premise for the false one in the subconscious. This can be accomplished by hypnosis. Then the reasoning of the conscious mind will be supported by subconscious agreement, rather than being negated by an obvious untruth in the subconscious which we recognize but cannot prevail against. Under hypnosis the conscious mind is inhibited so the truth can go directly to the subconscious without conscious censorship resulting from subconscious feedback. A knowledge of the interaction of these two minds is the most important factor in the intelligent use of self-hypnosis, and it is almost totally neglected in the meditation schools. It is great to be able to relax both your body and your mind through meditation and to expand your subconscious by passively observing it. But it is greater to be able to control it with positive life-affirming suggestions of your own choosing, and that is what a knowledge of the scientific principles of self-hypnosis can offer you.

THE SIX FUNCTIONS OF THE SUBCONSCIOUS

Before you start making changes in your subconscious mind, it is necessary to understand its nature and its functions. It was designed to be your servant, to fulfill orders given to it by your conscious mind. Since it was designed to serve, it makes a very poor master, yet most people allow it to control their lives. It consists of your desires, whims and emotions and the energy that drives you to satisfy them. Centuries ago King Solomon wrote, "For as a man thinketh in his heart, so is he."

The world "heart" of course meant the seat of the emotions, which is the subconscious, and he was certainly right. The force that drives you to conduct yourself in your usual manner is not what you think consciously, but what you think on a subconscious level. What your subconscious believes is the difference between success and failure, sickness and health and happiness and unhappiness. It has six vital functions:

1. It serves as a memory bank or computer. Here in the brain, with the help of billions of tiny inter-connecting nerve cells, everything we have ever seen, heard, smelled, tasted, felt or experienced in any way is permanently stored in a maze of memory patterns which, when activated, will feed back their information into the conscious mind. Nothing we have ever learned or experienced is, in strict scientific literalness, ever erased from these cell patterns unless a portion of the brain is injured or removed. This mind, or memory bank, is like a computer in more ways than one. When in hypnosis, we can recall memories of our early childhood that are completely forgotten by the conscious mind. We can also allow our subconscious to solve problems by feeding it all the pertinent information and then going into hypnosis while it compares this information with previously learned facts our conscious mind has long since forgotten. The answer comes to us suddenly, often while we are thinking of something quite different, and this process is what we often refer to as intuition.

Police departments in many of our cities are taking advantage of the mental computer concept of the subconscious by using hypnosis to help cooperative witnesses recall incidents their conscious minds have been unable to retain. One such case involved the witnesses to a robbery at a Montgomery Ward store in Eagle Rock, California. Two men with guns forced the counting room employees to lie down on the floor, while they scooped up fifty-two thousand dollars in cash and script. They were observed by a number of witnesses, some who saw them eating breakfast in the store cafeteria and others who saw them as they left the store. After several hours of questioning by the police, the chief of security for Ward's, Mr. Thomas Rhodes, suggested that Mr. Gil Boyne, a noted Hypnotherapist, be called in to interrogate the witnesses under hypnosis.

Several significant changes in testimony were elicited while the witnesses were in hypnosis. The employee who opened the counting room door when the robbers knocked had told the police the man who first approached him with a gun was clean shaven. When hypnotized, he recalled that the man had a several-days' growth of beard in the area of the chin, as though he were trying to grow a goatee. The witnesses who saw the men leaving the store said they had a black fibre-board case, and the employee who opened the door for them agreed. Under hypnosis they remembered a blue airline flight bag with two words stenciled in white on the back which was carried by the second man. Several other significant changes in testimony were elicited under hypnosis. One man remembered a license number on an automobile he had seen parked on the store parking lot as the store was opening two weeks previous to the robbery. This turned out to be a stolen plate, but his detailed description of the car and its occupants while he was under hypnosis led to the apprehension of two men, one of whom had sixteen thousand dollars on his person, which was confiscated. One of the men was on parole after serving a sentence for armed robbery.

In another case, a Chowchilla, California bus driver who had been kidnapped with twenty-six children was also able to recall certain numbers on a license plate while hypnotized, which he could not consciously remember. You know a lot more than you think you do! You just need to learn to operate your computer properly.

2. The subconscious controls and regulates the involuntary functions of the body, such as breathing, circulation, digestion and elimination. Since tension or stress inhibit these processes, they are responsible for the symptoms of psychosomatic illness. Hypnosis is the most effective method of

re-establishing their normal functioning because it can reach the controlling force. Hypertension can be controlled with the resulting lowering of blood pressure; indigestion and constipation can be eliminated; and many other psychosomatic diseases can be treated effectively by your direct orders to your subconsicous mind while in hypnosis.

We cannot emphasize too strongly, though, that a medical doctor should be consulted to be certain the disease is psychosomatic before proceeding with this method of treatment. A problem caused by bacterial infection could become critical without proper medical treatment. The proper suggestions while in hypnosis work in conjunction with medical treatment to bring about a much more rapid recovery, and this will be elaborated upon in a later chapter.

3. The subconscious is the seat of our emotions, and this accounts for its domination of the conscious mind. Since the emotions govern the strength of our desires, and since our desires govern our behavior, we are at the mercy of our subconscious unless we learn to control it. When we have conflicting desires, the subconscious one usually wins. The desire in a person's subconscious to conform to his religious or his ethical principles will inhibit a nearly as strong desire to commit some undesirable act. We always do the thing we most want to do, and our every contemplated act is the result of one desire outweighing another. Since the emotions are seated in the subconscious, and since the emotions govern the strength of our desires, it is obvious that it decides our course of action. Furthermore, if the conscious mind has done a poor job of programming it, the subconscious will do a poor job of regulating our decisions and consequent behavior.

As stated previously, the subconscious mind is incapable of discrimination and it believes anything it is told. If it could be made to believe you would die on a certain date you would surely do so. This death programming has been carried out successfully many times among people who believe in voodoo. If a believer knows that a doll representing him has had a pin stuck through its heart, he dies. We say a believer because the subconscious only accepts what the conscious mind believes.

An old man in a small city in Nebraska was convinced he would die if he took a bath. His greatest fear was that he would become sick and be taken to a hospital where he knew the first thing on the agenda would be a bath. His bones became brittle with age and one day he fell and broke his hip. He died, protesting, as they bathed him the next day in the local hospital!

Subconscious beliefs can cure or kill you!

4. The subconscious is the seat of the imagination. Many people say they have no imagination, but although they may have suppressed it, it is still there and active, often working against their best interests and well-being. As children we all have lively imaginations. Some stifle theirs as they emerge into adulthood after a number of painful confrontations with reality. They become afraid to imagine, in fear of more disillusionment or disappointment. But their imagination continues to work, and because it is undirected, it may turn them into extreme pessimists and prod them into imagining only the things they hate or fear. Life's failures are usually pessimists and defeatists, because their subconscious beliefs determine their actions. A belief in failure will result in failure.

If you need proof that your conscious mind cannot overrule your subconscious, try the following experiment and pit all your logic and will power against your subconscious, in this case your imagination. First, lay a ten-foot plank of wood, one foot wide, on the ground and walk the length of it. You will find this quite easy because your subconscious does not object. Now lay the same plank from roof to roof between two ten-story buildings and try to walk across, from one to the other roof. Your subconscious believes you will fall. Your conscious mind can reason that the plank is the same one you walked the length of on the ground, or that there is no difference where it is located, or that there is nothing to push you off or make you fall, but no amount of conscious will power or reasoning can overcome your imagination. If you try to walk the plank you will imagine you are going to fall, and you will. However, if you were hypnotized and your subconscious was convinced you wouldn't fall, you could walk between the two buildings with ease!

Creative imagination is one of the great secrets of success. All great artistis, musicians, engineers and architects draw their so-called talent from their subconscious minds. Most of the greatest works of art were created while the artist was in some form of self hypnosis. In this state, the imagination is dominant while the reasoning mind is dormant, and creative powers are at their peak. Mozart claimed his musical inspirations were formed like dreams, independent of his will. Coleridge created Kubla Kahn "in his sleep." Newton solved most of his mathematical problems while in so-called dreams. Goethe said his greatest poems were written while in a dreamlike state. These few examples represent the rule rather than the exceptions, and the list could go on and on. One contemporary portrait artist told us that after learning the mechanics of her work, she did her best paintings by letting her mind relax and allowing her hands to work for her. What she had learned academically seemed to combine with her imagination and her emotions, both of which are subconscious, to produce results she could not consciously conceive. Talent seems to be a combination of imagination and emotion, and an ability to control them.

Imagination can destroy you if it is not controlled. If you imagine your marital partner is unfaithful, you will act accordingly and probably ruin your marriage. If you imagine people don't like you, your responses will be such that they won't. Conversely, if you imagine yourself to be a friendly person that everyone likes, you will make friends easily. If you learn to control your imagination, it will work for you creatively. Since it is seated in the subconscious mind, hypnosis is the most practical way to harness its power.

5. The Subconscious carries out our habitual conduct. It manages and controls the activity we have reduced to habit. After you have learned such chain response activities as driving a car, dressing yourself or playing tennis, you no longer have to direct them with your conscious mind. Your subconscious takes over and does a better job of it, as you can easily discover by thinking of which leg to move next while you are running down the stairs. Don't try this experiment, because if you do you are certain to fall!

6. The subconscious is the dynamo that directs our energy, the energy that drives us toward our goals in life. It generates and releases this energy relentlessly, and if the conscious mind does not direct it, it is directed by chance or circumstance. Behavior is merely energy expressed. This energy cannot be destroyed, nor can it be created, but it can be directed. Since the subconscious constantly and automatically uses this energy to proceed toward a goal, unless you set a goal for it to achieve, it will either choose its own, or proceed toward a goal someone else has suggested. Without your direction it may strive toward illness, failure or some other destructive goal, and it always achieves what it sets out to accomplish. Here, again, is a case where the subconscious should be the obedient servant. It does not make a good master because it is incapable of choosing a proper goal. It is like a gushing fire hose. Properly directed, in the hands of a fireman, the force of the water quenches a fire and saves lives and property. But if the fireman lets go of the hose it can play havoc, knocking him off his feet and causing a great deal of damage.

The subconscious mind is not supposed to think, but to react to the thoughts you give it, and to carry out your orders. It is much easier to direct the subconscious than to let it push you around. It was intended to be the servant and you were intended to be the boss, and if yours has not pushed you toward success and happiness it is time you started giving the orders!

Sometimes we think we have no energy at all. We feel depressed and miserable. Yet without our knowledge, the subconscious dynamo is working at full capacity and continues to generate exactly the same amount of energy. Such emotions as hostility or anxiety utilize many times the amount of energy necessary to work toward a positive goal. Although we may not realize that hate, fear or resentment are present in our subconscious to a dangerous degree, our seeming "lack of energy" is often the result of these emotions draining the energy we need in our daily living. The amount of energy being generated in our body does not diminish. We simply channel it improperly.

The person who succeeds in his job or business and is drawing a high salary or making big money has chosen success for his goal, whether by conscious choice or by accident. Possibly he was fortunate enough to have had the idea planted in his mind by his parents or someone else he loved and admired as a child. Regardless of how the goal got there, he was bound to succeed. His full energy was used to achieve his goal and not wasted on fear or anger, either of which would have left him too fatigued to succeed by their excessive demands upon his energy supply. The man who always gives up when he gets to a certain point has failure as a goal. He was probably programmed as a child to believe he wasn't capable of amounting to much, or that he was incapable of handling responsibility.

Everyone is striving toward a goal, even if the goal is a life of indolence, and few people realize it because it is a subconscious drive. Your subconscious wants to receive guidance from your conscious mind because that is the way nature intended it. It will do exactly what it is told because this is its natural function. You can direct it toward success, better health, or anything else you desire and it will achieve it for you, even though you consciously forget what you ordered. Once an idea becomes fixed in the subconscious, it feeds it back into your daily behavior and makes you what you are. There is only one form of energy in the subconscious and it is neither positive or negative. It is up to you to direct it to work for you instead of against you. By using self-hypnosis, you can control your future by channeling your energy constructively.

THE FIVE PRINCIPLES OF CONVINCING
THE SUBCONSCIOUS MIND

1. The slow, hard way to reach and convince the subconscious is by repetition. Very few people have the tenacity to stick to this discipline long enough to obtain satisfactory results. However, radio or television advertising eventually plant ideas in the subconscious by repetition. You have probably found yourself selecting an item you haven't tried before because of constant advertising.

2. Identification with group or parent: If you are Irish you may have a subconscious desire to show off your so-called "Irish temper," which is merely an idea accepted because you are a member of that group. Again, you may have been told "You're just like your father" often enough to have accepted some of his habits as your own. This is subconscious programming by identification.

3. Ideas presented by authority figures are usually accepted as absolute truths by the subconscious. A person you admire and have great faith in can often change your subconscious beliefs, but this occurs more often during childhood than in the adult years. Friendly advice from someone you admire and trust is unlikely to convince your subconscious that you are going to quit smoking if you have a smoking habit. However, when scientists informed the public that cigarettes caused lung cancer and heart disease, a great many people quit the habit cold. This resulted from a combination of authority figure and fear, both of which can influence the subconscious.

A good example of an authority figure altering an adult's subconscious belief is a case in which a patient in a hospital had been hovering between life and death for two days. Being well along in years, he had resigned himself to death, and had asked that his relatives be brought in for last good-byes. A wise doctor who understood mental processes told the old man's wife, in a voice loud enough he was certain the patient could hear, that he had- finally gotten hold of a new wonder drug that would have the illness licked by morning. He then gave the old man two aspirin tablets. The following morning the patient was sitting up in bed, and he made a full recovery in the next few days. A subconscious belief had been changed.

4. Intense emotion opens up the corridor to the subconscious because the conscious mind is inhibited by emotion. If a child is badly frightened by a dog, he may fear dogs for the rest of his life, in spite of his conscious reasoning that the average dog is not only harmless, but friendly.

Mr. Gil Boyne, Los Angeles hypnotherapist, tells of an interesting case history in which a Mr. Rowe (not his real name) was referred to him by a doctor because of marital difficulties that were affecting his health. During his therapy sessions, he complained that his wife could not be convinced he loved her, no matter what he said or did. After some questioning under hypnosis, he recalled that during an argument on their honeymoon eighteen years before, he had foolishly told her he was sorry he ever married her. Because she was in the heat of anger at the time, her subconscious mind accepted the idea as true. Thereafter, although her reasoning conscious mind could understand that his every word and act proved her husband loved her, she still retained this subconscious conviction that he did not. Now hear the surprise treatment!

Mr. Boyne explained that since the false idea had been accepted by his wife while she was in the grip of intense emotion, it could be negated by replacing it with a conflicting idea during another intense emotional situation. He suggested that Mr. Rowe whisper, "I'm glad I married you" in his wife's ear during her next orgasm. Mr. Rowe followed this advice and his problem, and also his wife's problem, were solved. The subconscious was reached and convinced during intense emotion.

5. The fifth way to subconscious change is hypnosis, and this method is much more practical and effective than any other. Since the subconscious has no power of discernment, it believes anything it is told. This is one reason so many people have an unfounded fear of hypnosis. They have seen stage hypnotists tell a person, while he is hypnotized, that he is stuck to the floor. Since hypnosis allows a suggestion such as this to get past the conscious mind, which would surely reject it, and get through to the subconscious, the man thoroughly believes himself to be stuck to the floor, and is therefore unable to move his feet. Hypnosis is the fastest and shortest route to the subconscious, and if you learn to hypnotize yourself, you can tell it what to do, and then sit back and let it work for you.

THE RELIGIOUS ASPECTS OF HYPNOSIS

Most religions consider lies immoral and truths moral. A person whose character is founded upon lies, then, would be considered moral if he could readjust and accept truth. This is exactly what behavior modification is all about.

We are all born with a conscious mind capable of reason and discernment. This mind is limited in its capacity to attend more than one or two things at once, so we have a subconscious mind where concepts and ideas can be stored and drawn upon when needed by the conscious mind. This system worked very well for primitive man, whose needs and relationships were relatively simple. During the child's formative years, while his conscious mind was uncritical and therefore unable to properly direct his subconscious programming, he was protected by his parents and the elders of his tribe. He learned to hunt and fish, and to follow the tried and true customs of his group. His subconscious mind became the obedient servant of his conscious mind, and delivered correct information for his life style when needed. As civilization became more complex, with its industrialization and more complicated social structure, the child's subconscious programming also became more complicated, and conflicting opinions and abstract ideas confronted him daily. At this point, the programming method needed to be re-evaluated and changed, but it was not.

A young child accepts and internalizes ideas in much the same way as a hypnotized subject. The critical factor in a child's mind is undeveloped while in the hypnotized subject it is temporarily inhibited. So the child's programming in a more complex world became less accurate, with many distortions and misconceptions. As an adult, his subconscious was influenced by the material he had accepted earlier as truth, and that was influenced by material previously accepted, and so on, back to his formative years when he was incapable of discernment. It became a matter of the computer influencing its own programming with inaccurate data, leaving the adult believing untruths to be true and behaving accordingly.

Some readers may frown upon the concept of the human mind being a computer, and brand the whole idea as materialistic. But we are speaking only of the material part of the mind. There is no argument between science and religion about our brain. Whatever your religious conviction may be, it allows for the fact of material being on this earth and of a human brain capable of studying it. We are speaking to people of many faiths and we respect them all. Your chosen God has made you capable of observing facts, such as the rain falling, being evaporated by the sun, and then falling again. This is the interaction of material, and so is the working of our bodies.

Studying bodily material does not deny the existence of a soul. Since the soul is not material, but rather something spiritual, we leave each faith to its own version of soul's function and whereabouts. Although it is not impossible that mind may exist somehow and somewhere without body, we cannot. make use of it as living human beings without the material of brain matter. And this brain which allows us to be aware of mind can be removed piece by piece, by removing the tissue that causes it, the same as movement can be denied us by removing the limbs that do the moving, or even the tendons, muscles and nerves that operate them. If a great portion of a man's brain is removed, his reasoning will become no better than that of a frog. An accidental brain injury or a quantity of drugs can reduce a brilliant man to an imbecile or a moral man to a criminal. In this study of the human mind, we are dealing with something physical, not something spiritual, except as the two forces interact. Faith in your religion can be intensified by hypnosis and it can help you to live a better, more useful life.

History has recorded a continuing controversy over whether or not humans have "free will." Many great philosophers, including Schopenhaur and Einstein, have maintained that, since we are obviously products of our inheritance and our environment, our choices of action in any given situation are determined by our attitudes, desires and opinions, which are the result of those that preceded them, and then those that preceded THEM, and so on back to our childhood when our attitudes, opinions and resulting desires were implanted in our subconscious minds by our environment. We are obviously products of factors beyond our control, and to many this seems to deny that we have free will or moral responsibility. But we have the wherewithal to modify these previously learned behavior patterns by eliminating destructive or anti-social ideas while in hypnosis, and replacing them with positive, truthful concepts that will enrich our lives. Hence our free will.

It could still be argued that without accidental exposure to this or some other explanation of hypnosis, a man would be ignorant of his power to change, so is still a victim of his past, his will having nothing to do with his present state. The fact is, though, that man is born with the equipment necessary to change his character the same as he was born with legs to walk on. The fact that he misuses or does not use this equipment properly does not negate the fact that he has it, including that necessary for the exercising of the controversial free will.

Even with an understanding of the methods necessary to change for the better, and the accompanying free will to do so, many will find the idea of changing their minds abhorrent.

Such a person's ego will say, "I am John Jones, and I don't want to be somebody else." The ego guards this bundle of accidentally acquired ideas and opinions against change, and even rationalizes that a future of frustration and unhappiness is preferable to any reprogramming of this wonderful "me." There is also the type who says, "I wouldn't do any messin' around with MY mind." How often we see such people swallowing their tranquilizer pills or using alcohol to excess and insisting that they're "having a ball."

The fallacy in this ego thinking is that your real "me" doesn't faintly resemble the bundle of self-destroying habits and negative concepts it has degenerated into. You were born with all the requisites of perfect health, both mental and physical, and you can become a much more truthful representation of yourself by discarding lies and accepting truth as a foundation for your judgments. You were born right. Misinformation has brought about most of your difficulties. You have free will, and can be the happy individual you were meant to be! It's up to you.

MISCONCEPTIONS ABOUT HYPNOTISM

The average pre-conceived ideas about hypnotism are so far from true as to be ridiculous. Very few have knowingly availed themselves of its benefits because of superstition or fear. Meditators share some of its benefits, but deny its role in their practice. Most Christian Scientists bitterly oppose hypnotism, yet the founder of their Church first became interested in spiritual healing after being cured of paralysis by a "magnetic healer," as hypnotists were called during that period. Later, this "magnetic healer" was the anaesthetist at the first 'mesmeric' operation in this country.

There is nothing supernatural or magical about hypnotism, and there is not one documented case of harm coming to anyone as a result of its therapeutic use. Although its benefits are well established, it remains a misunderstood and often dreaded subject in the minds of the general public.

This resistance stems from our natural fear of any powerful force we do not understand. Ironically, there is a much greater danger in not understanding it. This force does not come from the hypnotist, but from your own subconscious mind, and if you do not control it, it controls you. Most of our physical ailments and mental depressions are the result of this uncontrolled power working against us when we could easily be using it to our advantage.

Hypnotism is neither metaphysics nor religion, although it does explain the miraculous cures effected by sincere faith healers. It is not contrary to the teachings of any of the major religions, and is, in fact, used in most of them. Any thought or idea repeated at length in solemn surroundings deepens faith by subconscious affirmation, and this is hypnosis. You are hypnotized to some degree every day of your life. While reading an interesting book, while watching TV, or any time when your conscious mind is absorbed, your subconscious is more vulnerable.

Fear of hypnotism is gradually giving way to acceptance by a more enlightened society. Doctors are finally accepting it as a valuable therapy in the treatment of the symptoms of psychosomatic diseases. Psychiatrists are supplementing psychotherapy with hypnotherapy, often reducing the therapeutic process to less than one eighth the time formerly needed for similar results. Since heavy case loads make the teaching of self-hypnosis impractical for the average medical doctor because of the time factor, they refer patients to qualified hypnotherapists who work under the doctor's supervision. Dentists are using hypnosis to relax apprehensive patients, and find, in the process, they need little or no anaesthetic for painless drilling or extraction.

It is encouraging to note that hypnotism is being accepted by these professional groups, and we predict that it will become a part of the curriculum in our public schools within a decade.

HOW IT FEELS TO BE HYPNOTIZED
You feel the same while hypnotized whether a professional hypnotist assists you or you do it yourself. Every muscle in your body becomes pleasantly relaxed and all tension disappears. This happens in various degrees from one hypnotic experience to another, until it becomes an entrenched habit pattern, after which you are able to completely relax in ten to thirty seconds. After your nerves and muscles relax, your mind also lets go, and although you can remain aware of the noises and activity around you, they do not disturb your tranquil, relaxed mood in any way. You are able to think if you desire to do so, but only an emergency will trigger such a desire, because you prefer to continue enjoying the pleasant, relaxed feeling of complete security and contentment. It feels almost like being awake while sleeping, or watching yourself sleep "in your mind's eye." You need not "pass out" or become unconscious. In fact, most people, after coming out of a hypnotic trance, don't believe they have been hypnotized. They say they enjoyed the experience immensely but they expected something much different.

You may remain conscious of where you are and what you are doing, but you just feel too relaxed and comfortable to want to think about it.

However, you can come back to complete conscious awareness at any time you choose. For instance, if the telephone rings, you can discard your trance and answer it without remaining in hypnosis during the conversation and then re-hypnotize yourself if you wish. No one has ever been unable to come out of hypnosis, and the sensational stories you hear about people who "can't get back out of it" are completely unfounded. A few neurotics who hate their life situations have been known to enjoy the pleasant relaxed state so much they refuse to awaken at another's command, but they can do so at any time they wish. If they refuse to return to the normal state of consciousness, they eventually go into normal sleep, and awaken as usual when rested, often wanting to be re-hypnotized. If you wish, you can be your own alarm clock, and decide upon the time you want to return to normal awareness before you hypnotize yourself. You will always come out of it at exactly the time you specify.

During the ten or fifteen-minute trance, both your body and mind become revitalized, and you awaken feeling physically refreshed and emotionally serene. You will have renewed energy without tension, and you will find it much easier to cope with the frustrations of daily living. You will look forward to your next hypnotic experience with pleasure.

One reason people have difficulty learning self-hypnosis is that they don't know when they are hypnotized. Because they expect something much different, they believe they have failed when they have not. There are various depths of trance which can be achieved, usually classified as the light trance, which is the feeling described above, the medium trance necessary for anaesthesia and age regression, and the deep trance which appears to be, but is not, deep slumber. The light trance is easily achieved by self-hypnosis, and it is sufficient for reaching and planting suggestions in the subconscious. The medium trance naturally follows with regular practice, and since it is a matter of degrees, you will find yourself in different depths during different sessions until you become conditioned to the point where you are able to choose. With practice, you can go into the depth you desire in ten to thirty seconds.

Here are some of the sensations you may experience while in hypnosis: Your arms or legs may seem to float a few inches above the floor, or they may feel heavy, as though they were sinking into the floor. They may seem to be in a different position than they actually are. You may lose conscious awareness of parts of your body, or all of it, and be conscious only of your mind. You may see strange visions or beautifully colored patterns of light. None of these sensations are harmful, and they are usually very pleasant.

Chapter II

SELF HYPNOSIS TECHNIQUES

PREREQUISITES OF SELF HYPNOSIS

Now that you understand the power of your subconscious mind and the role of hypnotism in reaching and influencing it, the next step is to learn to hypnotize yourself. The tools you will use are suggestion, concentration and imagination. If you have a good imagination you will find it easy to learn self hypnosis by any of the estabilshed methods included in this chapter. The ability to relax and just "let it happen" is important. If you try too hard you will become tense, and this is the opposite of what you are attempting to accomplish. If you take a skeptical "prove it to me" attitude, you will also impede your progress. Cooperate and you will get your proof.

Another thing to avoid is an analytical attitude. Analyzing will keep your conscious mind alert, and the whole object of hypnotizing yourself is to relax it. Analyzing also breeds doubt

Take A Trip Into Inner Space And Meet The Real You!

in the effectiveness of each step, and since hypnosis is a conviction phenomenon, doubt will slow your progress. We are assuming you want to hypnotize yourself or you wouldn't try to. You can't go into self hypnosis against your will, so you can't do it unless you follow the rules. You must avoid over-anxiety and skepticism and cooperate with the ideas suggested. If you follow directions, relax, and let it happen, it will!

HYPNOSIS THROUGH POST-HYPNOTIC SUGGESTION

The fastest and easiest way to learn self-hypnosis is by a post-hypnotic suggestion from a professional hypnotist. While you are in hypnosis, he will convince your subconscious mind that every time you perform some simple ritual such as counting backwards from ten down to one, you will go into hypnosis without his being present. This suggestion must then be re-inforced once or twice daily by re-suggesting the same thing to yourself while in self hypnosis.

Some need only four or five sessions with a professional while others with more resistance may need as many as eight or ten. Those who follow this advice and don't analyze, try too hard or play the skeptic will learn quickly and save money.

If you cannot find a qualified hypnotist to teach you self hypnosis, contact American Council of Hypnotist Examiners, 1147 E. Broadway, Suite 340, Glendale, CA 91205, (213) 242-1159.

PRELIMINARY SUGGESTIONS

Although the third chapter will explain auto suggestion in detail, there are a few suggestions that should be used each time you go into self hypnosis. The first is used to bring you out of hypnosis in case of emergency. The second is to insure you against going into hypnosis while driving a car or operating dangerous equipment of any kind. The third will make it easier for you to go into hypnosis in the future, and the fourth will awaken you at the time you specify, allowing you to decide in advance how long you wish to stay in the trance. This awakening technique will also insure you against any unwanted carry-over of induction suggestions. The state of hypnosis is so pleasant, some people are reluctant to come out of it immediately and show signs of hypnosis hangover which is characterized by slight drowsiness. The proper 'wake-up' technique eliminates this condition and brings you out of the trance feeling alert, vital, and completely rested.

You will find the proper wording for these suggestions in the third chapter under the heading "Supplementary Suggestions," and we suggest that you read them before practicing self hypnosis for any period of time.

COMMERCIAL HYPNOTIC TAPES

Another way to learn self hypnosis is through the use of recorded tapes or records. There is a pitfall here, because even though a few good tapes are available, there are many more being produced by quick-buck artists who are non-professional and often ignorant of the basic rules of effective suggestion. Before you invest money in hypnotic recordings, be certain you are dealing with a qualified professional. I recommend the tapes of Gil Boyne, which are the best I have found. A free Catalog of Self-Hypnosis Cassettes, Books and Courses is available from: Westwood Publishing Co., 312 Riverdale Dr., Glendale, CA 91205, (213) 242-1159.

After you learn the essentials of hypnotism and auto-suggestion, you can easily record your own hypnotic tape and tailor-make it to your individual needs. In this chapter you will find various induction methods which you may record by reading them into the microphone. The same is true of the deepening techniques. In the next chapter you will find instructions which will help you formulate beneficial suggestions in a manner acceptable to your subconscious mind, and these can be read into the microphone so you will hear them played back after you are in a receptive trance state. Then you may record an awakening procedure which is included in Chapter Three.

Always record these tapes in the second person, as though you were some other person talking to you. Instead of "I am becoming relaxed," say "You are becoming relaxed." Actually, your conscious mind is talking to your subconscious mind the same as one person talking to another.

This is one of the best and easiest methods of hypnotizing yourself and "getting through" to your subconscious without conscious interference. If you have or can afford a small cassette recorder, you will find it most convenient for this purpose, but any type of recording and playback equipment will do.

FRACTIONAL RELAXATION

This is one of the best induction methods for beginners. It takes a little longer than some other formulas, but it is a great conditioning technique for faster methods which can be more easily learned later. It relaxes the body completely, often to the point of partial or total loss of bodily awareness. Tension is released and the conscious mind drifts in and out of awareness of the surroundings, often viewing mental images of forgotten events from the subconscious. Here's how you do it:

Lie down on your back, arms parallel to your body, fingers loosely outstretched and palms downward. Separate the feet by eight or ten inches so that no part of your thighs are touching. Use a pillow if you wish, and make yourself as comfortable as possible. Remove or loosen clothing that binds you in any way and remove your shoes if they are tight. The idea is to get comfortable and relaxed.

If you are recording this procedure, use the second person throughout, but if you intend to use it without a recording, memorize it in the first person. We will give it here in the second person so it may be read direct from the book into the microphone. Start reading in a soft voice, rather slowly, and gradually slow down more and more, drawing out your words and pausing often between sentences. Your voice and the pace of your speech must suggest drowsiness and relaxation. Speak in a very slow monotone.

Now let's assume you are in the described position, and are listening to your voice coming from your recorder. Here is what you should hear:

Fix your eyes on a spot on the ceiling and take three long, deep breaths. Inhale, hold the air in your lungs for three seconds, and as you exhale slowly, you will relax all over. Now let's take the first breath. Inhale. (pause) Exhale—Sleep now. (pause) Now another deep breath, even deeper than before. Inhale. (pause) Exhale.—Sleep now. (pause) Now a third deep breath. Inhale. (pause) Exhale.—Sleep now. (pause) Now as your whole body begins to relax, and as every muscle and nerve begins to grow loose, and limp—your eyelids also become heavy and tired. They grow heavier and heavier, and will close now. The lids have become so tired and so heavy, it would be difficult to open them, but we have no desire to try because you want them to remain closed until I tell you to open them. (pause)

Now I want you to concentrate all of your attention on your right foot. Relax the toes of your right foot. Imagine they are like loose rubber bands dangling from your foot. (pause) Let this loose feeling spread back through the ball of the foot, and then all the way back to the heel. (pause) (Drag out the word 'all' and speak very slowly from this point on, pausing between all sentences.)

Now let this relaxed feeling go up into the calf of the leg. Let the calf muscles go loose—and limp—and LA-A-A-ZY. (long pause) And now, while your muscles and nerves are relaxing, let your mind relax also. Let it drift away, to pleasant scenes in your imagination. Let your mind wander where it will, as you go deeper—deeper—in drowsy relaxation. You are breathing easily like a sleeper breathes. All of your cares and tensions are fading away, as you go deeper—de-e-e-e-per into drowsy slumber. Every breath that you take—every noise that you hear—makes you go deeper, deeper, in pleasant, comfortable relaxation.

Now let the wonderful wave of relaxation move from your right calf up into the large thigh muscles. Let them go loose and limp. The right leg is now completely relaxed and comfortable. (pause) Now the left foot. The toes relax, the whole foot relaxes just as the right one did—limp and lazy. Let the feeling of pleasant relaxation go up into the left calf. Let the calf muscles go. Your legs are feeling heavy like pieces of wood. As you relax the left thigh muscles, they feel heavier and heavier, and you become more and more drowsy. Now as the wave of relaxation moves upward through your hips and abdomen, you let go more and more. Think of your abdomen as an inflated ball. You are letting the air out of the ball and it spreads out and relaxes completely. Stomach and solar plexus relax. Let them go—as you go further into deep—deep slumber. (pause) (slowly) The fingers in your right hand are now relaxing, and so is your wrist. Now your forearm relaxes. On up to your right shoulder—your whole right arm is relaxed and numb. You probably feel your fingers or your toes tingling. This is a good sign, so continue to go deeper. And now, just go on over, into a deep, deep hypnotic sleep. (pause)

The fingers on your left hand are completely relaxed. Your hand and forearm are letting go. Up, through your elbow, to your upper arm, relax. Now the left shoulder, let that go too. Loose, limp and lazy. Now relax all the large back muscles, from your shoulders all the way down to your waist—let them all go limp and loose. (Remember, plenty of pauses. Continue to speak softly and very slowly.)

Relax the muscles in your neck. Let your jaws separate and let the chin and cheek muscles go loose and rubbery. (pause) Now let your eyes go. Let them go completely—relax and feel comfortable and good. Relax the eyebrows too, and the forehead. Let the muscles rest. Back across the scalp—let the entire scalp relax—from the forehead all the way back to the back of the neck—all relaxed—all resting—all loose. You are now completely relaxed. Your body feels boneless. You are going deeper and deeper into restful hypnosis. Your mind is experiencing a wonderful feeling of tranquility. Your subconscious is now receptive to the helpful suggestions I am now going to give it.

(At this point the suggestion is given to the subconscious mind.)

After the suggestion is given, the supplementary suggestions outlined earlier in this chapter and detailed in Chapter Three are used, followed by the awakening procedure.

If you do not use a recorder, it is not necessary to memorize the text given here word for word. The idea is to start at one point on the body and relax each set of muscles by thinking of them individually. It is much easier to relax your finger, for instance, than to relax your entire body. When you concentrate upon relaxing one set of muscles at a time, and while doing so suggest sleep constantly, you will find it easy to expel the tension your body has a tendency to build up in to-day's way of living. Visualizing your toes, for instance, as loose rubber bands, or your legs as those of a rag doll, is also an aid in relaxing. If you don't memorize the exact text of the fractional relaxation technique, read it a number of times and use the ideas, framing them in your own words. You will find that the full text is seldom necessary. Most people are in hypnosis before the record or tape is half-finished. The words are not spoken, but just thought of, and the relaxation visualized, when used without a recording.

Fractional relaxation is a conditioning technique for those who are learning self hypnosis. If it seems long or cumbersome to you, remember that it will be unnecessary after a few weeks. When you become conditioned to hypnosis, you will be able to hypnotize yourself in a few seconds, so don't give up. Besides, there are many other ways in which you can hypnotize yourself, and if you are receptive to any of them, you won't wish to buy a hypnotic induction cassette, I strongly recommend those produced by Gil Boyne, Westwood Publishing Co., 312 Riverdale Dr., Glendale, CA 91205, (213) 242-1159.

COMBINING HYPNOSIS WITH MEDITATION

I am probably the first to advocate this method of induction, but I have found it to be very successful and easy to learn. Before you start, decide how long you want to remain hypnotized. For example, if you want to spend fifteen minutes, write the following sentences on a piece of paper: "Fifteen minutes after I go into hypnosis, I will awaken feeling normal in every way, wide awake and feeling wonderful. I will awaken in exactly fifteen minutes." Read this text at least six times, slowly and with emphasis. Think it and believe it. You will awaken at the time specified.

The next thing to do is make yourself comfortable. You may lie flat on your back or sit up in bed, resting against the headboard. Some get better results sitting in a straight-backed chair, feet flat on the floor, and hands palms downward on the thighs. Remove any clothing that binds you and try to relax.

Begin by taking a deep breath and tightening all the muscles in your feet and legs, up through your thighs and buttocks. As you exhale, relax the muscles and think "sleep now," as though you were telling the muscles it was time for rest. Now take another deep breath and tighten the muscles in the abdomen, shoulders, and arms. Double up your fists. As you exhale, let these muscles go limp and again think "Sleep now." It is now THEIR bedtime. Now take a third deep breath and tighten the face, neck and scalp muscles. Close your eyes tightly and make a grimace. Exhale, think "Sleep now," and release these muscles. Rest and breathe naturally for about thirty seconds.

Now pick a spot to fix your eyes upon. If you are lying on your back, find a spot on the ceiling. If sitting up, any spot slightly above eye level will do. If you can't find a spot, use a colored thumb tack, or paste a small piece of paper on the wall or ceiling. Stare at this spot. Don't let your attention waver and don't move a muscle while you take three more long breaths. Do it slowly, and allow about ten or twelve seconds between each breath. Breathe normally between these long breaths. Each time you exhale think the words "sleep now" and allow every muscle and nerve in your body to go loose and limp. Just let go completely. After the third breath is completed with its relaxation and a "sleep now," close your eyes and keep them closed until the awakening procedure.

Now, imagine you are at the top of a stairway. At the bottom of the stairs is complete relaxation. With each step downwards you will become more and more relaxed. Count the steps as you descend, "ten, deeper in relaxation, nine deeper, eight, deeper" and so on down to one, at which time you will be completely relaxed all over your body. After you reach one, imagine you lie down comfortably on the soft warm sand (or cool grass if you prefer) and continue to repeat "one, one, one" over and over to yourself. If other thoughts interrupt, and you find yourself forgetting to repeat "one," just start in repeating it again. During this period your subconscious mind will be receptive to suggestion. Whether you realize it or not, you will be hypnotized. Use the suggestion you wish your subconscious to accept, followed by the supplemental suggestions and the awakening technique.

It is important that you maintain the proper balance between hypnosis and normal sleep while using these techniques. A good rule of thumb is that if the awakening procedure brings you out of hypnosis, even though you feel as though you have been asleep, you have been in deep hypnosis. If you don't hear the awakening procedure and are inclined to drop off to sleep, you should combat this tendency by sitting in an erect position rather than reclining. If you do not go deep enough into hypnosis to become completely relaxed, you will find it easier with practice. It is possible, too, that another induction technique is more suited to your temperament. The next one employs your imagination only.

SELF HYPNOSIS BY IMAGINATION

First take the previously described three deep breaths. Each time, exhale slowly and think "sleep now," and as you let the air out of your lungs, relax every nerve and muscle in your body. Imagine it to be loose and limber like a soft rag doll. Whether lying down or sitting, pick up one of your arms and let it drop as though it were as heavy as lead. As it drops you will go deeper. Close your eyes, and relax all the muscles around them.

Now think of a beautiful scene. You are walking through a shady wooded area. You are barefoot, and the soft green grass feels good to your toes as you walk along. There is a gurgling mountain stream just ahead, and you pause to feel the grass against your feet for a few minutes more before stepping on the smooth, cool, flat rocks that border the stream. Your left foot remains in the grass while your right foot feels the smooth rock. Feel the grass between the toes of your left foot for a few seconds. It is soft and cool. Feel the smooth cool rock under your right foot. Sit down on the rock, and let your feet dangle into the cool, bubbling water. It is so pleasant and relaxing, you would like to stay awhile, but you see a galaxy of colorful flowers growing across the stream. They smell wonderful! There is a quaint rustic bridge downstream a few yards, so you get up and walk toward it. You feel a cool, refreshing breeze against your face, and notice a few fleecy white clouds drifting along through the clear blue sky. Crossing the bridge, you walk through the wild flowers and enjoy the sweet scent as you take a long breath and gaze about you. A hammock is stretched between two shady trees at the top of a sloping hill, and a narrow pathway looks inviting. You start up the hill and become more tired with every step you take. You are halfway up the hill now, and you want to stop and rest. But you decide to continue to climb. What a pleasure it will be to lie down in that hammock in that beautiful spot, and relax completely. Only five more steps now. You are very tired. Four more steps. You are tired but you can make it! Three more steps. Getting drowsy. Two more steps—almost there. One more step and then you can rest. You touch the hammock, and find it soft and inviting. You lie down in it and relax all over. Every nerve and muscle lets go and becomes limp, loose and lazy. You close your eyes and feel wonderful!

While you are in this relaxed state of mind and body, you are receptive to suggestion. This is entering hypnosis through imagination, and for many it is the fastest and most pleasant method of induction. Since exact wording is unimportant, you will only need to memorize the general story. If you prefer to be walking on a sandy beach, and climb a sand dune to the hammock, you can change the location. Just create a series of scenes you can feel. Call upon your sense of smell, touch, sight, and you might even add hearing and taste. You could hear songbirds, or taste cool spring water before you lie down in the hammock. Our series of scenes is just an example. If you record this induction, be sure to speak slowly and pause often between sentences.

THE GLUED FINGERS

Make yourself comfortable in a chair and stare at the thumb and index finger of your left hand. Put them together and imagine they are glued tightly. Push them together and imagine they are also bound with strong adhesive tape. The glue is drying and the finger and thumb are stuck tightly together. Stare at them and imagine they are becoming stuck tighter and tighter. Count from five down to one and after each count think "Stuck tighter." When you get down to one they will be stuck so tightly you cannot pull them apart, no matter how hard you try. The harder you try to pull them apart the more tightly they will stick together. Try to pull them apart, and as you try keep thinking the one thought, "The harder I try to pull them apart the tighter they stick." If you keep thinking this one thought to the exclusion of all others you will be unable to pull your thumb and finger apart. If you deviate and think "I'll bet I could pull them apart if I wanted to" your mind has wandered from the original thought and you are not following instructions. Think they are stuck and they will remain stuck until you say "now I can release them." When you say this you can easily separate them. At this point, continue into hypnosis by using any of the deepening techniques described at the end of this chapter.

THE "HEAVY ARMS" TECHNIQUE

Sit comfortably in a straight-back armless chair, close your eyes and allow your arms to dangle loosely from your shoulders down beyond the seat. Think of your hands only, and just be aware of them. Notice how they feel and how the blood rushes to them. You will notice how they seem to become heavier as you concentrate all your attention on them. Now imagine they are becoming more and more heavy. The longer they hang there, the heavier they become. They feel like they are made of lead. Imagine they get heavier, heavier and heavier. Imagine they are so heavy it would require a great effort to lift them. You are just too tired to lift such a great weight. Continue this thought to the exclusion of all other thoughts for two or three minutes, and then think "When I count from five down to one, I will be unable to lift my hands until I say 'now.' " Now count from five down to one in this manner:

"Five—my hands are so heavy I can't lift them. Four—heavier—and heavier. Three—I can't lift my hands. Two—my hands are so heavy I cannot lift them. One—My hands are so heavy I cannot lift them no matter how hard I try."

Continue to think "My hands are so heavy I cannot lift them no matter how hard I try" over and over again and at the same time try to lift your arms. If you have followed the instructions carefully, you will find it impossible to lift your arms until you say "Now," at which moment your arms will lose their heaviness and you will be able to lift and use them normally. As you say "now," lift your arms and place your hands, palms downward, on your thighs and relax all over. Continue with your choice of the deepening techniques described at the end of this chapter.

THE SEMAPHORE METHOD

Sit comfortably in a straight-back chair and place your feet flat on the floor. Extend both arms in front of you at shoulder height with palms facing each other, and close your eyes. Imagine a big blue balloon is tied to your right wrist by a long string. It is filled with lighter than air gas and it pulls upward on your arm. Visualize the balloon clearly, rising above your right arm, pulling it upward. Tugging and pulling, as your arm goes higher and higher. Think of your arm rising, a little more and a little more as the balloon tugs on it. Develop this image clearly in your mind, but don't consciously move your arm. Don't hold it back either.

Now think of your left arm. Imagine a heavy weight is hanging below it, tied to the left wrist by a thick rope. Picture the weight as a large cast-iron dumbell. Think about how heavy the weight is, and how it pulls downward on your left arm. Picture your left arm as being very heavy—so heavy you can hardly hold it up. Feel it going downward, lower and lower, pulled by the heavy weight.

Go back and forth mentally between the two arms and the two ideas. Your right arm is being pulled upward by the balloon and your left arm is being pulled downward by the heavy weight. After several minutes of alternating between these two arm conditions, open your eyes. If you have concentrated sufficiently, the right arm will be several inches above the left arm. At this point let your arms go limp and fall to your thighs. As they rest there, palms downward, take a deep breath and as you exhale, relax all over. Continue with one of the deepening techniques described at the end of this chapter.

If you fail to get the expected results in any of the last three procedures, it is not because you can't be hypnotized, but rather because you are not in the habit of concentrating on one thing or one idea. Sometimes it takes a little practice. Try the stuck thumb and finger again and play a little game with yourself. PRETEND you can't pull your thumb and finger apart when the time to test them comes. Continue to concentrate on the thought "I cannot pull them apart no matter how hard I try" while you pretend you can't. You will be surprised how quickly the game will become the real thing.

DEEPENING TECHNIQUES

When you have attained a slight degree of hypnosis it is often desirable to deepen the trance in order to relax the mind and body to a more suggestible state. Although suggestions, when administered properly, will be accepted by the subconscious mind during a light trance, difficulty in retaining the trance is sometimes encountered. Individuals vary in their abilities to attain the deeper stages of hypnosis, and those who do not go into a satisfactory trance state after using one of the induction methods described earlier in this chapter will find the following deepening techniques helpful.

COUNTING BACKWARDS

Take three deep breaths, and each time you exhale relax your whole body and think the words "Sleep now." (After you follow this procedure a number of times, you will become conditioned to the words "sleep now" and you will be able to go into hypnosis by this method alone.) About twenty seconds after you exhale the third breath, start counting backwards, starting at 100, and after each number think "Sleep deeply." As soon as you miss a number or can't remember which number comes next, stop counting and relax your mind by repeating the word "one" over and over until you forget to repeat it and find yourself thinking of something else. When you realize you have strayed from the discipline, start repeating "one" again. This will deepen your trance to the maximum degree possible for you at that time. It will always deepen it to some extent, even the first time you use it. If you find it too easy to count backwards and don't forget which number comes next after going down to fifty, try counting backwards and repeating "Sleep deeply" after every other number, or if this is still too easy use the "sleep deeply" after every third number. For example, "One Hundred, sleep deeply. Ninety-seven, Ninety-four, sleep deeply. Ninety-one. Eighty-eight etc. etc." This is one of the best of all the deepening techniques for self induced hypnosis.

THE ELEVATOR

Imagine that you are seated in a comfortable chair in an elevator. You are on the tenth floor, and you are seated so that you can see the hand on a dial that points to the numbers of the floors as you pass them. The elevator moves very slowly, so the hand moves slowly from ten down toward nine. You are nearing the ninth floor and you become quite drowsy. As the elevator moves downward, you go deeper and deeper into hypnosis. When you reach floor number one, you will be more pleasantly and comfortably relaxed than you have ever been before. Now you reach and pass the ninth floor and the dial is slowly moving toward eight. You become more and more relaxed. Every sound that you hear, every easy breath that you take, makes you go deeper—deeper into drowsy relaxation. The dial passes eight. Going down, deeper and deeper. Don't let your eyes stray from the dial. Every muscle and every nerve relaxes as you see the hand pass seven. So sleepy. So perfectly comfortable. (pause) Now we reach the sixth floor. All of your cares and tensions are fading away as you go down—down further into drowsy relaxation. The hand is now at five. Halfway down. Let go more and more. Let your mind relax also. Think only of the hand on the dial as it moves on down to four. (pause) The hand is passing four and as it passes, you let go again. Tension has almost completely disappeared. (pause) Three. Almost there. So relaxed. Soooo Sleepy. The hand reaches two. Now you are almost down to the first floor where you drift off into a pleasant, dreamy hypnotic sleep. When the hand reaches one, think the words "Sleep now" and you will pass on over into a wonderful state of relaxation. You will feel so comfortable, so completely loose and limp all over your body, you will be deeper than ever before. Now the hand moves downward—down—down to number one. "Sleep now." Just let go completely, and enjoy the perfect, peaceful relaxation of a deep hypnotic sleep.

This deepening technique gives excellent results when used as a recording, but the ideas can be utilized without mechanical aid by imagining yourself seated in the elevator and visualizing the hand moving gradually from ten down to one. If you choose to use this method, read the text aloud at least three times just before you hypnotize yourself and concentrate upon the meaning. Don't try to memorize it. Visualizing the moving hand on the dial will prompt your subconscious to feed back the most important elements in the text if you have followed instructions and read it carefully several times just prior to induction.

REPETITION AS A DEEPENING TECHNIQUE

When you have attained a light state of hypnosis, you can deepen it by repetition of the same induction or portions of it. For instance, you may open your eyes, and looking straight ahead, take the often-used three deep breaths, thinking "With each breath I will go deeper into hypnosis." After you exhale, think the words "Sleep now" and relax further. After a few minutes, repeat the procedure, and you will eventually reach your maximum depth. Or you may open your eyes and think "As I count from five down to one I will go deeper and deeper, and when I reach one I will close my eyes and relax completely." When you open your eyes, stare straight ahead and don't look at anything in particular. When you close them, at the count of one (you have counted from five down to one) allow your body to relax. Think of it as heavy and pleasantly numb. This deepening technique can also be repeated if necessary.

HAND LOWERING TECHNIQUE

After securing a light trance by any of the induction techniques, raise your left arm above shoulder level, double up your fist, and tighten all of the muscles. Make your whole arm as stiff and rigid as a steel bar, and think of it as hard and heavy. Because it is so heavy, it will gradually start to descend after a while. When it seems to be moving downward, let it drop to your side and let this be a signal to go deeper into hypnosis. As your arm relaxes, let your whole body relax also. This is a rapid method of deepening the trance and it may be repeated as often as necessary to attain the depth desired.

OTHER METHODS OF REACHING
THE SUBCONSCIOUS

In this chapter I have given you the self hypnosis techniques I believe you will find easiest to learn. Chapter Five will explain meditation in its various forms and other related mind expansion modalities, all of which have merit. At this point, though, since you are now capable of hypnotizing yourself, it is important that you know how to construct a suggestion in a manner that will influence your subconscious mind. Before going further in your experiments with mind expansion, I interrupt with the following chapter so you may familiarize yourself with the basic principles of suggestion.

Chapter III

EFFECTIVE AUTO SUGGESTION

STRUCTURING YOUR SUGGESTION

By its very nature the subconscious mind must obey suggestions as though they were orders. During hypnosis, while the conscious mind is inhibited to a great extent, it is possible to reach the subconscious with these suggestions, or orders, without their being influenced by conscious interpretations of related memories and fixed ideas.

When approaching the subconscious without the benefit of conscious reasoning, you must remember that the subconscious reasons deductively only, and certain rules must be followed in the wording of your suggestions. By structuring suggestions correctly you can put this great source of energy to work for you, carrying out your orders without use of will power or conscious effort of any sort. Your subconscious is much better at regulating your behavior than your conscious mind, because nature intended that as its function. Most of

Ask In The Right Way
And You Shall Receive

---

your behavior is on a subconscious level and when your conscious mind interferes with it, it is usually rather frustrating. Just try to think of "no lions." Think of anything else, but don't think of lions. The more you think "Don't think of lions," the more sure you are to think of them. This is the law of reverse effect. The harder you try consciously to do a thing your subconscious is supposed to do, the less the chance of success. The person with insomnia can go to sleep only when he stops trying. So use the following principles in structuring your suggestions, relax and let your subconscious do its job. It will never disappoint you.

1. THE MOTIVATING DESIRE MUST BE STRONG. If you hypnotize yourself and tell your subconscious to make you dig a hole six feet deep on a hot day you won't get much cooperation, because it knows you don't have a real desire to

do that much hard work in the hot sun. However, if you tell your subconscious you want to earn more money, and mean it, it will work day and night, even while you sleep, to grant your wish.

Before you start to write your suggestion, choose a reason or a number of reasons why you want your suggestion carried out. This must be a counter-emotional motivator to replace the behavior pattern you are intending to eliminate. If you are over-eating, your present emotional motivator may be the enjoyment you derive from tasting certain foods. The emotions that might be chosen to replace this habit could be a desire for better health, a pretty figure, looking better in clothes, or becoming more attractive to some particular person you care for.

Start your suggestion with your motivating desire: "Because I have a strong desire to have an attractive, slim figure and because I enjoy wearing a size nine dress, etc. etc.," or "Because I want to feel physically fit and enjoy vibrant health, etc."

2. BE POSITIVE. If you say "I will stop eating too much" you are REMINDING the subconscious that you eat too much, thereby suggesting the very idea you want to eliminate. If you say "My headache will be gone when I come out of hypnosis" you are suggesting a headache. To frame these thoughts positively, you should say, "I am always well satisfied with a small meal. I enjoy eating only at meal times, and after I have eaten food amounting to approximately four hundred calories, I push my plate away and say that's enough. I get up from the table feeling entirely satisfied and enjoy the resulting loss of weight." If you wish to suggest that your headache will go away you should say "My head feels better and better. It is clear and relaxed. My head feels good. It will continue to feel good after I come out of hypnosis, because all of the nerves and muscles are rested, relaxed and normal."

Never mention the negative idea you intend to eliminate. Repeat and emphasize the positive idea you are replacing it with.

"What is expected tends to be realized." This is the law of mental expectancy. If you expect to toss and turn instead of going to sleep at bedtime, you will do just that. If you expect to feel terrible the next morning you will get what you expect. Job, the hard-luck figure of Biblical times, stated it correctly: "For the thing which I so greatly feared is come upon me, and that which I was afraid of is come unto me." Every time you say "I have trouble going to sleep at night," you reinforce an already fixed idea in your subconscious mind. You are playing the role of the person who can't go to sleep. Luckily, you have the ability to change the script, but be certain that your suggestion does not include your present image of yourself. The subconscious can only respond to mental images, and the idea is to form new mental images. Think of yourself acting in a more satisfactory way, whether it is awakening in the morning feeling good or sleeping comfortably at bedtime. And let us reiterate: Never mention or think about the idea you are eliminating. Self hypnosis is positive thinking in its most practical form.

3. ALWAYS USE THE PRESENT TENSE. Never say "Tomorrow I will feel good" but rather "Tomorrow I feel good." This may seem strange to your reasoning mind because you have learned to speak of the future in the future tense. But since your subconscious is an emotional, feeling mind it responds to the present only. When you read your suggestion, don't just say the words you have written. Think them, imagine them and see yourself acting out the suggestion. If your goal is to eliminate stage fright, feel yourself standing before a large crowd, speaking with poise and confidence. When you use your imagination you are in direct contact with the subconscious, and that is what you are trying to influence. Your self image has a great deal to do with your success or failure in life. If you want to be a success, visualize yourself as

a success. If you picture yourself as a person who can't get anywhere in life, you will fail. Even if you don't use self hypnosis, the image you have of yourself will determine your future, but with hypnosis you can accelerate the change to any self image you wish to imagine. See yourself as you want to be or visualize your goal as already accomplished, and then hypnotize yourself. The saying "Wishing will make it so" is scientifically correct in this case, if you follow the ground rules. It should now be clear why you must always use the present tense in all of your suggestions. Imagine what you are suggesting is true, not some time in the future, but now! This is the only kind of communication your subconscious mind will understand and act upon.

4. SET A TIME LIMIT. Although you must picture your goal as having already been reached when dealing with the subconscious, your conscious mind, which can reason, knows you can't do some things overnight. If you fracture your leg it won't mend in ten minutes, although all pain may be eliminated by hypnosis. If you want to become an expert bowler, even your subconscious can't grant your wish immediately. So you must set a realistic time limit. Find out how long it usually takes a leg with a similar fracture to heal. Set your time at one-half of that amount and let your subconscious go to work. Or let an expert show you how to bowl, and imagine yourself, in your suggestion for self hypnosis, doing exactly as he tells you to do. You will be amazed at the results! Remember, your subconscious is a goal-striving mechanism, and once programmed toward a goal it never stops until it achieves it. Set a realistic time limit, and you will find the goal is usually reached well before the time you set!

5. SUGGEST ACTION, NOT ABILITY TO ACT. Don't say, "I have the ability to dance well" but rather "I dance well, with ease and grace."

6. BE SPECIFIC. Choose a self-improvement suggestion you are anxious to carry out, and work with that one suggestion until it is accepted. Don't suggest a number of things at once. You may alternate suggestions at different self-hypnotic sessions, but never work on more than two or three at once, and never more than one during a session. While learning, it is best to start with suggestions that are easier to carry out so that you can see more immediate results.

7. KEEP YOUR LANGUAGE SIMPLE. Speak as though your subconscious were a bright ten-year-old. Use words the average ten-year-old would understand.

8. EXAGGERATE AND EMOTIONALIZE. Remember, your subconscious is the seat of the emotions, and exciting, powerful words will influence it. Use descriptive words such as wonderful, beautiful, exciting, great, thrilling, joyous, gorgeous, tremendous! Say or think these words with feeling.

9. USE REPETITION. When writing your suggestion, repeat it, enlarge upon it, and repeat it again in different words. Embellish it with convincing adjectives. When you are satisfied that your suggestion is attractive and influential, repetition is again necessary during self hypnosis sessions. The more often you are exposed to an idea, the more it influences you. Repeat your suggestion daily until it becomes entrenched in your subconscious.

While a subject is in hypnosis, he will accept almost any suggestion from the hypnotist because his entire attention is focused upon that one thing. The former experiences that would ordinarily come into his mind (associated memories) are not remembered. THE BRAIN WILL ALWAYS SEND OUT A MESSAGE TO ACT UPON ANY SUGGESTION, UNLESS CONFLICTING SUGGESTIONS INHIBIT IT. That all forces act along the line of least resistance is a fundamental law of matter. This is also a law of mind, since mind is merely the activity of matter—the result of stimulating nerve cells. The oftener a card is creased, the more likely it is to bend in the same place again. And the oftener a suggestion is acted upon by the UNCRITICAL MIND, the more certain the suggested response is to repeat itself.

EXAMPLE OF A FINISHED SUGGESTION

First you must select a goal. In this case we will assume you have difficulty going to sleep at bedtime, and want to relieve the condition. The first thing you must do is choose a positive motivating desire, which of course would be the desire to get a good night's sleep and a desire to awaken in the morning feeling refreshed and rested. So you start your suggestion:

"Because I want to get a full night's sleep, and because I want to awaken in the morning feeling completely refreshed, rested and full of pep and energy, each night as I retire I relax every muscle in my body by taking three deep breaths. After each breath I say "Sleep now' and let every muscle and nerve go loose and limp. After the third breath I am so completely relaxed I immediately drift off into a deep, restful slumber which remains unbroken until morning. Only an emergency awakens me, and if this happens I return to bed after attending it, and go to sleep within sixty seconds. It is easy for me to relax and go to sleep because I expect to sleep. Throughout my sleep, I am contented and pleasantly relaxed.

"I always relax completely upon taking three deep breaths, and at bedtime I always go to sleep as I relax. I sleep soundly and comfortably and without effort. Throughout my sleep I feel calm, contented and relaxed, and I carry this calm, contented sense of relaxation over into my waking state. I always awaken at my usual rising time, and feel wonderful! Completely rested, alert and cheerful! I thoroughly enjoy my deep restful sleep, and at bedtime I just take three deep breaths and think 'sleep now' after each one, and I go to sleep automatically. All of these thoughts come to me when in hypnosis; when I think of the code word 'Bedtime.' "

Now observe how this follows the nine principles of suggestion.

1. First, it gives a reason: Your desire to sleep at bedtime. "Because I want to get a full night's sleep, and I want to awaken in the morning feeling refreshed."

2. All thoughts are positive. Sleepless nights, insomnia or staying awake are not mentioned. Only sleep, rest and comfort are emphasized.

3. The present tense is used throughout. Even the future is treated as the present.

4. A time limit is set. "After the third breath I immediately drift off into deep, restful slumber."

5. A type of action is suggested, that of going to sleep. "I can go to sleep" is not used, but rather "I go to sleep."

6. The suggestion is specific and right to the point.

7. The language is simple enough for a ten-year-old child to understand.

8. Exaggeration is used, as well as emotion-bearing words. "Completely relaxed," "Every muscle in my body," "wonderful," "contented," "without effort," "thoroughly enjoy," "completely rested."

9. Repetition is used generously.

THE SYMBOLIZED SUGGESTION

If you do not use a recording device which will give you the suggestion verbally while in hypnosis, you must symbolize your suggestion. Note that the example suggestion ended with the code word "Bedtime." This could be changed to "deep slumber," "sleep," or some other word or phrase which symbolizes the content and feeling of the suggestion to you. The symbol must create a mental image or a strong feeling of your actively carrying out the suggestion, in this case the taking of three deep breaths and relaxing every muscle and nerve in your body and going to sleep. Choose the symbol which symbolizes these things to you.

If you are overcoming faulty concentration, you might use the code words "Think sharp," "Free Mind" or even "Concentrate." If you want to lose weight you might symbolize your suggestion with "Size nine" or "Physically fit." It is important that the symbol reminds you of the suggestion.

The reason you must use a symbol to represent your suggestion is that while in hypnosis the conscious mind is dormant, a condition necessary to reach and arouse your subconscious. If, then, you use your conscious mind to detail the suggestion to your subconscious, you arouse it from its inhibited state and defeat your purpose. Hypnosis differs from sleep in that the conscious mind is under your control even though it is dormant, and you can think of a code phrase or symbol without disturbing your trance.

First, write out your suggestion, following the ten principles outlined earlier in this chapter. Choose a symbol that best describes or represents the suggestion to you. Then read it aloud at least three times. Read it slowly and with feeling. Concentrate on its meaning. If you are in a place where you cannot read it aloud, read it four or five times to yourself.

Now you are ready to hypnotize yourself. You should be conditioned by now to use the three deep breaths, each followed by the words "sleep now," but if you are not, use any of the methods outlined in Chapter Two. As soon as you feel the deep relaxation of hypnosis, think the symbol, and the symbol only, and then let your mind relax and drift. Don't try to think of the wording of the suggestion. Let your subconscious absorb it in its own way. A few phrases from your suggestion may float through your mind, or you may just feel a sense of your suggestion being an accepted truth. Allow visions of yourself with your suggestions a reality to enter your imagination, but without conscious effort. Impressing the suggestion upon your nervous system by reading it aloud several times has turned on the ignition. Thinking the symbol has activated the starter and set the wheels rolling. Hypnotizing yourself has opened your subconscious to suggestion.

Some find it helpful to hold the written suggestion in one hand while in hypnosis, or if they are inclined to drop it when in the relaxed state, tape it to the hand. This serves as a reminder, while in hypnosis, that the suggestion is to be considered to the exclusion of all other matters.

SUPPLEMENTARY SUGGESTIONS

There are a few suggestions which should be incorporated in every hypnotic session until they become fixed habits. "I awaken immediately in case of any emergency, alert and completely normal in every way." "I automatically achieve the proper balance between the conscious and the subconscious, so that all of my suggestions are readily accepted." "I go into hypnosis more quickly and easily every time I practice it." "I stay completely free of hypnosis while driving a motor vehicle or operating dangerous machinery." "I awaken in exactly fifteen minutes," or set your own time limit.

THE AWAKENING TECHNIQUE

If you use a recorder you can record the awakening at the close of your recording. If you do not use a recorder, either memorize the following in the first person or use your own language with a similar message:

"Now it is time for you to return to normal consciousness. You feel wonderfully rested. I will count to five, and as I do you feel vitality and energy surging through your body. You are wide awake at the count of five. ONE. You are waking up now. When you awaken, you feel full of pep and energy. TWO. More and more awake! More and more awake!

You feel refreshed and perfect from head to foot, normal in every way. THREE. You feel as though your eyes had just been bathed in cool spring water. You feel physically perfect and emotionally serene. FOUR. You feel wonderful in every way! Refreshed and full of vigor, but perfectly relaxed and calm. You feel good all over! FIVE. Eyes open! Wide awake now. Take a deep breath, stretch, and feel good!

If a recording is used, the induction should be in a slow monotone as previously stated, the suggestion should be given in a crisp businesslike tone, and the awakening should be louder and spoken forcefully and with enthusiasm. A gradual transition should be made between the induction and the suggestion so as not to startle the subject out of the trance.

HYPNOTHERAPY

There are times when a symptom or a habit you consciously wish to eliminate plays a vital purpose in your life adjustment. You may, without realizing it, be dependent upon the symptom or habit for a defense against some traumatic situation you have chosen to forget. In some such cases your subconscious may have difficulty in accepting the desired suggestion. If the habit or sympton is causing enough discomfort or unhappiness to justify its removal, your doctor may refer you to an hypnotherapist. He will regress you to the time of the original trauma while you are in hypnosis, uncover the event you fear to face, and allow you to relive it and view it from an adult standpoint. Then, with nothing to hide from and nothing to fear, you can easily eliminate the habit or symptom with auto-suggestion and self hypnosis. The subconscious memory has been brought back to the realm of conscious thinking and re-evaluated.

In most cases, however, symptoms or habits can be eliminated without hypnotherapy, even though they are the result of some such repressed incident or memory. The success of these cases is probably correlated with the degree of intensity of the original trauma.

Thousands of forward looking psychiatrists have added hypnotism to their behavior conditioning techniques during the past few years and have found this radically abbreviated form of deep therapy saves them many months of sessions. Sometimes when a phobia results from one of these single traumatic incidents which have been forgotten by the conscious mind because of the mental anguish its memory produces, recalling the event will reduce or neutralize a phobia. This is the psychoanalytic approach, and it often takes many expensive sessions with the psychiatrist and with questionable results. More often, though, the phobia persists in spite of the painful remembering and acceptance of its original cause. In these cases treatment by hypnotherapy will decondition fear by reciprocal inhibition. This is accomplished in much the same manner as Pavlov's conditioning technique. The patient visualizes himself performing the activity he fears in his imagination while in hypnosis. He gradually neutralizes the fear by establishing a new attitude toward it.

THE CONDITIONED RESPONSE

Pavlov, a famous Russian scientist, suspected that many of our responses to average situations were inappropriate. His experiment, in which he conditioned a dog to salivate to a bell proved his point. He caused a hungry dog's saliva to flow by presenting it with meat, and at the same time rang a bell. After a number of repetitions, the bell alone caused the dog to salivate. The natural response of salivating to food had been transferred to an artificial one—the bell. Pavlov called this a conditioned response.

Many of our attitudes and feelings are the result of such conditioning during our formative years. For instance, a child who sees a rabbit for the first time during a storm, and is simultaneously frightened by a clap of thunder, may transfer her fear of the noise to fear of the rabbit. Later in life the child may feel uneasy around rabbits, or even fear them. Sometimes this conditioning may generalize into a dislike of men with beards, or of women in fur coats. All of this conditioning is internalized and becomes absolute truth to us once it is accepted by our subconscious.

We may be bored during a long lecture or recital, and, without realizing it, transfer our feelings to the hall or auditorium in which it is held. Later, any room decorated in the same colors or having the same general appearance may depress us. Our lives are full of conditioned responses which might have been avoided had we been trained in psychology during our grammar school years. It is obviously unnecessary for us to feel depressed when exposed to certain colors or decorating schemes because we were bored at a lecture one evening many years ago. Behavior is built upon suggestion, and reaching your subconscious mind with new powerful and positive concepts is the only way to overcome your past programming.

Chapter IV

CONTROLLING DESTRUCTIVE EMOTIONS

EMOTIONAL MATURITY

Most human beings mature physically, some of them mature intellectually, but few of them mature emotionally.

A distinguished scientist may have memorized volumes of material and may be a respected authority in his chosen field, but he may be completely unreasonable if angered during an argument. His I.Q. may be 160 or more but his emotional growth may be that of a peevish child. How common it is to see professors who have never left the academic community thinking and acting like the youths with whom they have never lost contact, and exaggerating idealistic theories beyond practical limits! A well-rounded adult matures physically, knowledgeably, intellectually, and emotionally. Most of us do not mature emotionally, and frustration and unhappiness are the result. Consider a sporting event in which a questionable point is scored. The participants and spectators of the scoring

Every Emotion Effects You Physically

side will agree almost to a man that their team scored legitimately. The opposing team and their followers will be positive that the score was not made. Neither group knows which viewpoint is correct but they let their emotions think for them. If they wanted the truth they would have suspended their judgement until the facts were made clear. Emotional thinking is seldom truthful thinking.

Locke divided people into three groups in regard to how they think:

1. Those who seldom think at all. These people follow the example of those they have faith in and save themselves the trouble of thinking. They are capable only of "surface" conversation such as what they did yesterday or what some other person did or said.

57

2. Those who allow their appetites or passions to govern their reason. These people refuse to recognize probabilities that run cross-current with their desires or interests. They deceive themselves by keeping their beliefs in "logic-tight compartments" through which no argument to the contrary, no matter how obvious, is allowed to pass. Ruled by their ignorant emotions they constantly cause trouble for themselves and their families by inhibiting the brain which was designed to help them.

3. Those who sincerely use their brains to reason things out, but whose reasoning is based upon their own interpretations, which are the result of their previously conceived prejudices. Without possessing a full view of all of the facts pertaining to a question, and assuming that their own concepts pertinent to a question are true, they arrive at a false conclusion which, to them, seems logical. They then fit this new conclusion into their scheme of reasoning as a basis for future wrong judgements. Even the most scientific thinkers have difficulty escaping from this group.

In contrast to the average individual's way of gathering information and forming conclusions, the scientist conducts systematic observations and experiments, and considers only the resulting evidence. He accepts as fact only that which can be proved. In this way he frees himself from preconceptions and prejudices and forms his conclusions upon the true findings of precise observations. When the truth is learned, it is tested openly by other scientists, especially by those who had formed other opinions about the probable outcome of such investigations, and the results are recorded as scientific evidence. Unlike the average opinion or superstition, a scientific fact can be verified by anyone wishing to perform the recorded experiment himself.

It may be more comfortable for the moment to think with our emotions instead of our conscious, reasoning mind, but we usually pay a heavy price for our short-lived comfort. The subconscious mind is supposed to be the servant and the conscious mind should control it. An emotionally mature person learns to reject the emotions that are detrimental to his well-being, and nurture those which are conducive to his health and happiness. The negative emotions include anger, hostility, hatred, jealously, anxiety and resentment. The positive emotions include love, friendship, kindness, forgiveness, generosity, sympathy, tolerance, and charity.

The negative emotions make us unhappy and sick. The positive emotions keep us happy and well. It is just as simple as that!

Every emotion has a physical effect. Most of them were important to man during various stages in his development. But uncontrolled emotions are like uncontrolled doses of medicine. A drop of a powerful drug may save a life that a pint of it would kill. Certain emotions cause the glands to secrete chemicals which make us sick and depressed.

I will treat the worst offenders separately in an effort to convince the conscious mind of their destructive nature. Then I will offer an affirmation which will convince the subconscious mind as well, while in self hypnosis. With repetition this will facilitate control of the emotions without conscious effort, and allow you to choose which emotions you wish to control.

ANGER

Anger is the most destructive of all our emotions because it lies hidden unrecognized in many other causes of maladjustment. In guilt we are angry at ourselves. In hate we are angry at the object of our hatred. In self-pity we are angry at the situations or people that frustrate us.

Anger may be overt, but more often it is insidious in its many disguises. Expressed or suppressed, it accounts for most of our misery. No one can become so emotionally mature as to completely free himself of anger, but by minimizing it we can lead much happier lives. When we succeed in shaking off the fetters of hostility, our anger is replaced with pity, and possibly even amusement, at the emotional naiveté of those who take hostile thrusts at us.

From the time of birth we are exposed to anger-provoking situations. From the comfort of the womb we are forced out into changing temperatures and hostile sounds. We are slapped smartly on the bottom and laid on a dry cloth instead of the moist membranes we have become accustomed to. As we grow older we are forced to drink from a hard, cold glass. Our anger mounts as we are forced to delay natural functions until we are placed on a toilet seat, and to accept other responsibilities such as dressing ourselves and tying our own shoes. As more and more restrictions are heaped upon us, our frustration and consequent anger increases. As teenagers we crave freedom from parental control without wishing to accept the responsibility of self-support.

Those who are able to accept these challenges and adjust to them as they grow are better conditioned to accept the responsibilities of adult life without the limitations anger places upon their daily activities. Those who continue to rebel against the inevitable forces of nature and the necessary restrictions of group living become increasingly hostile toward others and toward themselves as well. We may not be able to entirely overcome our desire to be taken care of like babies, but for our own health and happiness we must learn to accept the world for what it is and not allow our anger to add to the problems we must face.

Expressed anger usually arouses anger in the one we address, and their hostility intensifies our own. Soon a vicious cycle is established, and logical argument is displaced by foolish exaggerations and name calling. Because of this, most people learn to suppress their anger, and it festers like an infested sore, causing chronic physical changes in the body that lead to illness and depression. The nervous tension resulting from suppressed anger is the frequent cause of gastro-intestinal disorders, asthma, ulcers, high blood pressure, headache, skin eruptions and heart attacks.

Once while I was interviewing a successful fighter, I asked him if he had any advice for young boxers. "Never get mad," he said. "Let the other guy get mad, and he'll fight like a fool while you're the master of the situation."

It is seldom that emotional responses are preferable to intelligent responses in a civilized society. During anger the adrenal gland becomes over-active, and although the glandular secretion adds to our bodily strength, it inhibits the functioning of our brain. Although we may be able to run faster when frightened or muster more strength when angered, we are unable to think as clearly. In our way of life we seldom have to run in fear or fight for our lives as our cave dwelling ancestors did. So, rather than becoming angry or afraid, either of which emotion confuses the brain we must try to control it with, it is more desirable to AVOID becoming angry or afraid. But first we must recognize the fact that we have anger, discover the source of it and understand its destructive nature.

Years ago the excuse for intemperate outbursts of anger was "I never saw a good horse without a temper." But a horse was born an animal and will aways remain an animal. We are born animals, but with the potential for rising above animal behavior and becoming humans. And only as we overcome our animal emotions do we become less animal and more human.

A great deal has been written about relieving hostility by screaming, slamming doors or telling someone off. And granting you are filled with hate and hostility, this is often advisable. It is a relief to scratch your eczema, and to take cough syrup for pneumonia too, but it won't cure anything. Yell and slam doors until you are relieved, and then get vaccinated to avoid further "infection"! You don't have to suffer with hostility if you don't accept it in the first place.

The heavy-drinking, brawling hero of many movies who enjoys fighting and throwing chairs through expensive mirrors is an example of the general misconception of manhood. Such stories tend to portray the emotionally immature brute as a sex symbol. But if animal behavior signifies manhood, a hog should be the envy of every man, and we should try to emulate its conduct.

Those who repress anger are in worse trouble than those who are emotionally immature. They realize that it is an unsatisfactory method of dealing with most problems, but instead of learning not to become angry they learn to conceal it. Since anger uses energy that must be released, this energy surfaces in roundabout ways, and causes even more physical or mental suffering than it would had it had a direct outlet.

A man who doesn't dare talk back to his boss often finds an excuse to become angry at his wife when he returns home from work. A woman may feel angry because of her seemingly thankless job of keeping the house clean and taking care of the children while her husband is spending his evenings out with the boys. Rather than accept the thought of anger she suffers headaches or ulcers.

In these cases anger must be recognized and dealt with. The man who is angry at his boss might find his total life situation more acceptable if he suffered through the unemployment period that could result from quitting his job and looking for a better one. Another alternative would be to gain self confidence through self hypnosis and auto-suggestion, and thereby gain a better relationship with his boss. The woman might try to establish a better relationship with her husband by explaining her problem to him and asking for his help and advice, while still understanding his desire to enjoy himself. Communication without anger and without pointing the finger of guilt often obtains understanding and cooperation, even from self-centered people, if handled in a friendly "seeking your advice" manner. She should seek every course open to her to improve her situation and remove the source of her anger. Then she must accept her remaining hardships as her fair share of the frustrations we all have to face. Happiness can be hers despite the seeming difficulties through modification of her attitudes. There is a great deal of good in life to counter-balance the bad, and although we are all forced to accept some of each we can enjoy a minimum of the bad through improved thought patterns. We can change the inner environment if we can't change the outer.

HOW TO DEAL WITH ANGER CREATIVELY

You will not become angry at people if you understand them emotionally as well as intellectually. Recall, we are all products of our inherited physical attributes and experiences. The key thought of your new attitude must be this: You would do exactly the same things as the person who angers you does if you had been born with his body, his same glandular activity, and had experienced the same influences in the same order as he has throughout his life to this moment. So consider the injustice and also the futility of becoming angry at someone who, because he was born with different equipment than you, and has had different influences and experiences than you, acts in a way you yourself would act if you were in his shoes. You might justifiably disapprove of the cannibal for his customs, but anger would be inappropriate, besides doing your own body more harm than good.

The criminal chooses his course of action in exactly the same manner as the ethical or religious person chooses his. His early experiences have shaped his subconscious in such a way that his conduct is not what law-abiding people consider proper. Others with similar environments may admire him and emulate his conduct. Although we may not prefer such individuals as companions we are certainly wrong in hating them, because their desires and lack of inhibiting desires are not of their own choosing. This does not suggest that criminals should be coddled as so many psychologists believe. Those who prey on others should be separated from those who cooperate to achieve group happiness, until they can be rehabilitated. Some violent criminals probably could never be rehabilitated and should be permanently removed from society. They can't help their desires and lack of inhibitions, and punishment should not be the object of their confinement.

A rabid dog can't help being rabid, either, but we can't have him running the streets.

Nothing could sound more foolish than a judge who asks a young hoodlum, "Don't you want to grow up to be a respected member of our community?" The boy may say "yes," hoping for more lenient treatment, but secretly he considers the judge an old fool. He wants to conform to the customs of his street gang and their approval and admiration are his principal desires. These shape his other desires. If he had been raised in Father Flannigan's Boys' Town, he would prefer to conform to the customs of boys who have been rehabilitated. Should we hate him because he was not? We should rehabilitate him, but our present attempts in institutions or in his own neighborhood are usually unsuccessful.

It is a fact of nature that although man has free will to choose his course of action, he cannot choose his desires unless he understands auto-suggestion. Since the strongest desire always directs his actions, and since he cannot be blamed for his desires we cannot logically be angered at his behavior any more than we can be angered at the weather. He is acting exactly as you would act if you were he.

Anger can cause a great amount of unhappiness, and it can cause many forms of illness. It is usually unjustified. When you are angry your brain is inhibited and, therefore, you are reduced to something less than your human potential. Use the following affirmation with self hypnosis, and impress the desirability of tolerance and understanding upon your subconscious mind. You will feel at peace with the world, at peace with yourself. Repeat it until it is burned into the subconscious.

AFFIRMATION FOR CONTROLLING
ANGER AND HOSTILITY

Because I want to live happily and harmoniously with other people, and enjoy good health physically and emotionally, I have a feeling of peace and tolerance toward everyone. I like people and people like me. I realize that each personality is a product of heredity and experience. I know that if I had been born with someone else's body, and had gone through the same experiences in the same order as they, I would act exactly as they do. Therefore, I accept others as they are, and when they do things I disapprove of, the only emotions I feel are sympathy and understanding. I am in complete control of my emotions at all times, even under what others believe to be stressful conditions. This gives me a feeling of great satisfaction. I feel and express only the good, healthful emotions of love, kindness, sympathy and tolerance toward others. I love other people for their good qualities and I forgive them for the acts I disapprove of, because I know they are doing what anyone else would do with their same body, experience and levels of awareness.

I am a friendly and loving person, and I have a kind word and a warm smile for everyone. For this reason I am well liked. I accept others as they are. I know that my pleasant disposition often starts a chain reaction of pleasant feelings in others, and they treat others better as a result. This makes me feel good. Others like and admire me for my understanding and forgiving nature. I am happy because I know the key to happiness is love and understanding, tolerance and sympathy. I harbor these beneficial emotions and reject all others. I am a better, more admirable person for my ability to smile at those who are angry, and I find it easy to think clearly and choose the proper words because I am serene and relaxed. I sympathize with people for their bad qualities, and I love them for their good qualities. I am in complete control of my emotions, and only the good and healthy ones are present in my mind. These healthy emotions feed back into my daily living and keep me happy and contented. I enjoy being tolerant, understanding and forgiving. I now forgive everyone for anything they have done. I like people and I like myself. I am a tolerant, good person, sympathetic and understanding. I am relaxed and comfortable around other people because of my loving attitude toward them. I like people and I understand people. My sub-conscious mind absorbs all of these ideas and feeds them back into my daily living. My subconscious mind is where the emotions reside, and it guides me in selecting good healthful responses. I am a friendly, warm, loving person. I accept others as they are. I am in complete control of my emotions at all times. I radiate the good, healthful emotions and reject all others. I am experiencing personal growth with each day that passes.

I like myself and I like people.

(If not recorded): These ideas and concepts are symbolized by the word Tolerance (or any other word or words that represent these ideas to you).

SELF PITY

A belief in Santa Claus or the Easter bunny is appropriate to the very young but would be abnormal in the teenager. Believing that the world should be a utopia is an idea appropriate to teenagers whose ideals exceed their experience. College students living on allowances are often indignant at the inequities in a world they have yet to challenge. But by the time people reach the age of responsibility they should have learned that the bitter and the sweet are inevitable parts of their future and they must learn to accept them both. Acceptance is one of the keys to happy living and positive action is the other. Change what you can, then accept what you can't.

The self pitier gets stalled emotionally at the teen-age level, and expects too much of the sweet and none of the bitter. He regards his own trouble as unique and he believes he is getting more than his fair share of life's hardships. To him, his troubles seem sufficient cause for his unhappiness. But if he would question several strangers he meets on the street, he would find most of them are suffering with problems as bad or worse. Problems, hardships and disappointments are inevitable for all of us, but those who let their minds dwell on the negative side of life invite more of the same. We cannot deny the negative side of life, but we can learn to accept it as the opposite side of the coin. The other side is the happiness we get if we reach out for it.

Love and friendship are courting you on all sides if you project your own. It has been man's nature from his most primitive days to desire the approval of others in order to receive good treatment and help when needed. No one is more depressed than a person in solitary confinement. So the hostility you may encounter in some people is usually not dislike of you as a person, but self defense against possible disapproval or hostility on your part. Consider the liar, the braggart or the person who can always better your story. These people are complimenting you. They are telling you, in their own emotionally stupid way, that they are worthy of your friendship. They are saying, "Aren't you impressed with all of my accomplishments? Wouldn't I make a good friend for you?" People everywhere are crying out for friendship, and are often alone and angry because of their failure to find it.

The self pitier is self-centered. He must learn that he and his desires are not the center of the universe. He has his troubles and others have theirs. No one can expect to be satisfied with everything in life, but we can learn to enjoy living by programming our subconscious mind to be happy with what we have, or to get what we want. It is natural to WANT something or someone to be different than they are, but to be UNHAPPY if they are not as you desire them to be is self-destructive. So don't expect to be completely satisfied with everything. No one has ever been and no one ever will be.

Many self pitiers use suffering as a defense. They believe people will feel sorry for them and therefore like them better. These people are often inclined to resist hypnosis as a remedy for their unhappiness and refuse to help themselves. Remember that happy people draw friends like magnets while self pitiers drive them away. Others can be amused at the inequities of life while self pitiers suffer. When fate plays one of its pranks, a well-adjusted person can do as Omar Khayyam suggested:

"But leave the wise to wrangle, and with me
The quarrel of the universe let be:
And in a corner of the hub-bub couched,
Make game of that which makes as much of thee."

You may go Omar's route and change your inner environment, or you may change your outer environment, or both! The affirmation at the end of this discussion on pity will help you to change what you can and accept what you can't.

PITY FOR OTHERS

Many people suffer exaggerated emotion over other people's troubles. They read the papers about the suffering in the world, and even though they themselves are well fed and comfortable they become depressed because the world is so cruel to others. Often this stems from a feeling of guilt for having more while others have less. More often, though, it is genuine sympathy carried to a self-destructive degree. Of course these people should feel sorry for people who are less fortunate than they, but not to the extent of hurting themselves. They are also important human beings, and they owe their body and mind proper care. Depressions slowly destroy it. You have probably been taught that the more sympathy you have for others the more admirable you are. It seems to be a part of being a better person. But sympathy alone won't help anyone, and it will hurt you if you sympathize on a destructive level.

Let's say you see twenty people suffering, and you are not in a position to help them in any way. Is it better to add yourself to this group which will then be twenty-one suffering people? Help others where possible instead of crying for them, but if you can't do anything about the situation, accept it. A depression can only hurt you, and it can't help anyone else. And being self-destructive certainly is not high-moraled conduct. It is normal to sympathize with others in trouble or in need but it is neurotic to let it make you gloomy or depressed.

AFFIRMATION FOR SELF PITY

Because I want to live a happy, healthy life, and because I want other people to like me and enjoy my company, I accept life as it is and I accept people as they are. I am enjoying living more each day. I like people and I forgive them for being different than I expect them to be. I realize that it is natural for people to disagree with each other and with me in many ways because of their varied environments. I realize that there is a great deal of good in most people even though I happen to see the side I disapprove of. I love people for their good qualities and forgive them for their mistakes.

I know the world has a lot of good to offer, and I concentrate on the good things. Therefore I get the good things. I am happier with every day that passes. I have great anticipations and I reach out for happiness. I find happiness because I anticipate it. I now wear a happy expression. I look happy because I feel happy. I smile when I greet my friends. They like me better because I have a new, enjoyable personality. I feel better every day because I am happy. Being happy and contented with life brings me better health. I am relaxed and contented, and my bodily functions are working perfectly as a result. I accept the world as it is and go along with the tide. As I relax and accept life, my health improves daily and I feel great! Happier every day. Healthier every day. I enjoy life. I enjoy people.

(If not recorded): These ideas and concepts come into my mind when I think of the words "Happy life."

AFFIRMATION FOR EXAGGERATED PITY
FOR OTHERS

Because I desire to do right by keeping my body and mind healthy, and because I want to live as nature intended, I have deep sympathy and understanding for the hardships of others, and help others to the extent that it is practical for me to do so.

I lead a happy life, and I share my happiness with others. I keep a happy frame of mind because my happiness starts a chain reaction in others. I can't help everyone who has troubles, but I help those I come in contact with by being pleasant and happy. Happiness is contagious, and I expose everyone possible to happiness. I know that happiness comes from within. I know that people can be happy in spite of many misfortunes. I am contented, and I keep my sense of humor in spite of anything that happens. I have inner peace. It is my duty to keep a contented, satisfied attitude even while striving for better things for myself and others. A peaceful mind is the key to personal health and personal growth. My nerves and muscles are relaxed, and I enjoy perfect health as a result of my happy attitude toward life. I treat my body as I should by relaxing and enjoying life. My attitude is one of tolerance and understanding.

(If not recorded): These concepts and ideas are symbolized by the word "Contentment" (or by any other word or words that symbolize these ideas to you).

GUILT

Guilt is a form of self-abasement. We punish ourselves by disrupting the vital life functions of the body, inviting illness and depression. American Indian women of certain tribes used to slash their legs to the bone to show grief when their mates were killed in battle. They made their situation worse and the whole tribe was handicapped by trying to transport them. Punishing ourselves because we feel guilty about something is equally ridiculous, because we become morose and irritable, and eventually we become incapacitated with illness.

If you have read the preceding chapters, you must understand that your actions are caused by a long series of causes and effects in your past, and your character is determined by inheritance, environment and education. If this were not true, you would be wearing a ring in your nose as is customary with those in a different country who have had different training. A child is born with inherited physical characteristics, but he is not born with inherited conscience, attitudes, morals. The conscience is governed by the strength of the desire to conform to the customs of the group. A tribe in another country refuses to recognize a young warrior's manhood until he has killed a member of a neighboring tribe. So the young man's conscience is not at ease until he has committed what we would consider a cold-blooded murder. If we had been born in his environment we would feel proud and happy after our first killing. So guilt is a realtive matter.

We are raised to think and act the way our opinions and desires dictate, so how can you logically feel guilty about what your experiences in our present culture have made you? If you have feelings of guilt, the act you feel guilty about is now past experience. Feel sorry about what you have done, but not guilty, because the experience, like all experiences, caused a slight change in your total personality. Your character is not your past, but rather what the past has made you. You are not exactly the same person you were ten years ago. The minute you recognize a mistake and have desire not to repeat it, you have advanced your education and the quality of your chacacter, and your mistake must be considered an experience that served to improve the quality of your future behavior. So don't feel guilty about behavior you wouldn't repeat. If you feel sorry about it you have become a slightly better person as a result of your act. You are automatically forgiven, because you are not exactly the same person who committed the act.

Whether you believe in Jesus Christ as a deity or merely as a historical figure, he was obviously a very intelligent man. It is a matter of recorded history that he realized the men who were crucifying him were products of their inheritance and experience. He prayed: "Forgive them, Father, they know not what they do."

Most religions teach forgiveness, and if your God can forgive you, you should be able to follow His example and forgive yourself. If you have to hate, hate the act that made you feel guilty and don't repeat it. A good rule of thumb is: If you wouldn't do it again, you are forgiven. To burden yourself with guilt is to misuse your brain by punishing those billions of hard-working little cells that make up your body. You don't gain forgiveness by ruining the body you were entrusted with.

Many people harbor guilt because they can't face their true feelings of hatred or anger. A girl who wasn't treated fairly by her parents may have mixed feelings of love and hate toward them. The norms of our society tell her she shouldn't hate her parents, yet some parents act in such a way that they don't deserve love. She buries her guilt in her subconscious and it causes phychosomatic illness because it is not recognized and dealt with. In severe cases guilt must be resolved through Hynotherapy, but more often we can use introspection to see ourselves as we really are. If you have guilt feelings about your attitude toward someone, consider looking at things as they actually are, rather than how you were taught they were supposed to be. Maybe your parent, or some close friend, deserve your dislike or distrust. Bring the hatred out in the open and admit it to yourself. Then hypnotize yourself and use the affirmation for anger. This will negate your anger, reduce your feelings of guilt, and make you a much healthier and happier person.

Guilt feelings are so painful to the conscious awareness it may be difficult to lure them out of your subconscious. But when buried there without the reasoning processes of the conscious mind, they become exaggerated and intensified, and can be relieved only by suffering. Since the subconscious controls the vital involuntary functions, it is an expert in handling the torture rack, and it metes out punishment out of all porportion to the crime, often causing complete disability. Like a splinter, it hurts until it is removed.

The most ludicrous form of guilt is the "If I hadn't done so and so it wouldn't have happened" type, yet it is very common among the emotionally naive. A woman and her husband get a late start for a dinner engagement because she spends a few minutes extra getting dressed. A drunk driver crosses the double line and hits their car head on. She comes out of it with minor injuries but her husband is killed. Her burden of guilt is heavy. "If I hadn't been late getting dressed it wouldn't have happened," she thinks. This is soap opera stuff. To feel guilty over some normal thing you have done preceding a tragedy is illogical and silly. By this type of reasoning a man shouldn't leave his home to go to work, because his wife might have an accident and be unable to get to the phone to call a doctor. Then he would feel guilty because he wasn't there to help her.

Harboring guilt serves no good purpose. It doesn't right wrongs and it doesn't help anyone or anything. If you are using guilt as a form of self punishment you are breaking the laws of nature. Everyone makes mistakes, and you have a right to be wrong. But you don't have a right to punish a healthy body and make it sick, even if it does belong to you. Think how many crippled people would appreciate having a body like yours. To hate yourself is neurotic, to forgive yourself is divine. Following is an affirmation to abolish guilt:

AFFIRMATION FOR FEELINGS OF GUILT

Because I want to have a healthy mind and a healthy body, I hereby forgive myself for all things I have done in the past.

I throw a heavy yoke off my shoulders as I forgive myself. I forgive myself, and everyone else, because I know we are all products of our inheritance and environment. I want the best for everyone as well as for myself. I am a loving person and I live a happy, contented life. I feel a great feeling of peace and tranquility and forgive myself, and start with a clean slate. During the day, as I go about my daily routine, I feel a wonderful new sense of freedom. Now and then a little thrill runs up my spine and I suddenly remember that I have good feelings toward everyone. I like myself and people sense my self-respect and like me better for it. I radiate love, kindness and forgiveness for everyone, and for myself also. I am a good, loving person, and I deserve happiness and respect. I forgive everybody, and I forgive myself because forgiveness is good, and right. I feel a great sense of freedom as I forgive myself and I am at peace with the world.

(If not recorded) These ideas and concepts are symbolized by the word "forgive."

ANXIETY

If you are deeply depressed you need professional help and should see a competent Hypnotherapist, who will through the use of hypnotism ascertain the cause of your depression in a few sessions. The most intelligent person is usually totally unaware of the cause of his depression, and by age regression the hypnotherapist takes him back in his memory to the time when some traumatic event occurred which he finds too painful to accept in his conscious mind. It is then dealt with in a way that neutralizes the effects of the incident, and the cause for the depression disappears.

Genuine sadness is a normal reaction to the death of a loved one or to any other great loss or disappointment. Fear is normal when life or happiness is threatened. The intensity of these emotions diminishes with time and must be accepted as a part of life everyone must occasionally endure. But exaggerated fears without reasonable cause, instead of diminishing with time, often increase in intensity and generalize into incapacitating anxiety and phobic reactions. If a boy is walking across a railroad bridge and he sees a train approaching, fear would be a healthy reaction. It would stimulate his adrenal and other glands, transfer the blood from his stomach and intestines to his heart, increase his blood pressure, and enable him to run faster and reach a point of safety. The short-lived emergency is then over and his vital functions resume their normal activity without having harmed his body.

Fear in its chronic form keeps the body in a constant state of emergency alert and causes the physiological processes to function abnormally. Anxiety is a sickness of the mind, and a sick mind invariably results in a sick body.

Anxiety is often the result of a habit of exaggerating the possibility of danger out of proportion to its probability. It is remotely possible that you could be harmed in an earthquake if you live in California, or that you could be hurt in a tornado if you live in the central plains states. If you live near a river you could be caught in a flood. Normal people accept the risks for what they are, possible but remote, and don't let them interfere with their lives or their happiness. Neurotics literally worry themselves sick, treating each possibility as a probability. The resulting apprehension causes a constant state of incomplete digestion, high blood pressure, rapid pulse and general disruption of the vital bodily functions. This inevitably leads to some form of psychosomatic illness.

Fear must be followed by action. The purpose of stepping up bodily activity is to insure greater temporary strength with which to overcome the fear-producing challenge. Anxiety is fear that finds no outlet. It is needless to sound the alarm and prepare the body for action every time we think of an earthquake or a tornado when in all probability we will spend a lifetime unharmed by either. There is no action we can take to prevent them, so the worrier is racing his motor at full throttle while his car stands parked, using all the energy he needs for his daily living, and wondering why he is tired out and sick.

A good example of exaggerated emotion that affects many is fear of flying. Thousands of times daily airplanes take off and land with a near-perfect safety record. The stripes on the sleeves of many grey-haired pilots attest to their having flown daily for twenty to twenty-five years without a mishap. Statistics show flying in scheduled commercial airlines to be safer than driving an automobile. Yet fear causes many people to drive for days rather than use air transportation. In dealing with the conscious mind, the chances of being harmed must be compared to the chances of not being harmed. You will still have your fear, because you won't be convinced emotionally, but you can correct that by self-hypnosis.

But let's reason with the conscious mind first. If an airline pilot can fly practically every day for twenty years, why should you expect an accident on that one day you decide to fly? The person dominated by such fears will say, "When I fly, that's just the one day an accident is likely to happen." Is there any logical reason to believe this? He thinks he is so important that ninety other people will be harmed just so that he can be right! By this reasoning he should be afraid the motor will drop out of an airplane, go through his roof, and hit him while he sleeps. It is possible, and he thinks he is important enough to have it happen to him! I sincerely hope I haven't added another worry to someone's pet fears. My sense of humor gets me in trouble sometimes, but I'd hate to have it cause anyone else any problems!

Recently I taught a Mrs. J. to hypnotize herself, and the principles of structuring a suggestion. A month later she came to me with this story. "My husband travels a lot, and he always uses air transportation. I often wanted to go with him, but every time I got on the plane I was scared to death. I sat with my eyes shut tight on the take-off and landing, and held on to the arms of the seat. That is, until the last trip! I hypnotized myself every day for three days before we left and played my tape while in the trance. On the tape I had recorded such suggestions as: 'I enjoy riding on an airplane. I like to look out of the window on the take-off and see the houses getting smaller and smaller. I get a big thrill out of the thrust upward and I am alert and interested in the whole procedure. I enjoy seeing the tops of the fleecy white clouds, and watching the rivers curling about in a way I have seldom seen them. Then the landing is fun. The houses get larger and larger and it is a genuine thrill when I feel the wheels touch the ground and we roll along the runway. I get a real thrill when I fly and I love to do it!' I got on the plane without my usual apprehension, and looked out of the window during the take-off just to see if I could. I actually enjoyed watching the houses get smaller as we gained altitude and felt no fear at all. My husband called my attention to the fact that my palms weren't wet, as they usually were. I am so happy, because I have conquered my fear of flying!"

Like Mrs. J. you can reprogram your subconscious mind with positive, confident thoughts and conquer unreasonable fears. Fear comes from within, or everyone would fear the same things. One person will face a situation with confidence and bravery while another will succumb to fear and panic.

Abnormal fears are usually the result of unfortunate past experiences and often they can be remembered. Mary B., at the age of four, was in the barn gathering eggs with her mother when she was startled by her mother's shriek of panic. She followed her into the back door of the house and saw the sink overflowing and the kitchen floor covered with water. "I forgot to turn the faucet off!" her mother yelled hysterically as she splashed through the water to the sink. Although her mother had reached out of all proportion to the seriousness of the situation, Mary was emotionally scarred by the seeming helplessness and panic of the one she depended upon for security. However, this was not an event too painful to remember, so Mary didn't find it necessary to block it from her conscious mind.

Later, while in elementary school, she lived in constant fear that the town water tank, which was located on the school lot, would overflow and drown her and all of her schoolmates. At that time she didn't connect her fear with the overflowing sink incident, but as an adult Mary now remembers many such incidents in which her mother was panicked by fear. Her conscious mind understood but her subconscious mind had been conditioned to worry excessively, in spite of her understanding of the underlying cause. She has now learned self-hypnosis, and after six weeks of reprogramming her subconscious with positive, life-affirming concepts she feels as though a weight had been lifted from her shoulders, and she is enjoying life more than she had ever dreamed possible.

SELF-LIMITING FEARS

1. FEAR OF CRITICISM. This crippling fear touches nearly every one of us. We want to be liked and admired, and

think we have to be perfect to merit love and affection. However, no other person will agree that we are perfect, or that anyone else is perfect, so everyone comes in for their fair share of criticism, whether they hear it or not. When we learn to accept ourselves and others as imperfect, we are much happier facing the truth. "It takes a good man to admit when he's wrong," and it is a good feeling when we can build greater self-respect by being able to do so. When we learn to admit our short-comings we will become (and feel) superior to others who are constantly on the defensive. We can relax and take criticism with good humor, and people like us better. Even when we feel the criticism is not justified, we learn that the other person thinks it is, and can judge our actions better in the light of this knowledge.

2. FEAR OF FAILURE. This fear limits the accomplishments of many talented, capable people. The most common response to fear of failure is refusal to try. A life of mediocrity is the inevitable result. Others give up prematurely. Those who bravely try in spite of their fear often develop psychosomatic symptoms, to make failure impossible. A young artist joined the staff of an advertising agency, and her first assignment was a cartoon of a fat man being chased by a leopard. She was more adept at serious illustrations but she had training in cartooning and could have fulfilled the assignment successfully. But her fear of failure caused a temporary inability to lift her right arm. The pain was severe and real. Immediately after another artist completed the drawing, the pain left and her arm became normal. She considered her disability a coincidence because her conscious mind refused to accept the truth, that she was afraid of failure. But her subconscious mind was defending her against an exaggerated fear stimulated by a subconscious reaction. Repeated fear stimuli over a period of time may completely incapacitate people and leave them chronic invalids.

3. FEAR OF REJECTION. This fear possibly accounts for more disturbed personalities than any other. A child who is made to feel unloved and rejected develops feelings of worthlessness. If his parents—whose opinion he believes to be unerring—think he is no good, then he must be worthless. This resolves itself into self-hate, which is so intolerable some escape must be found. Some develop physical illness, by which they punish themselves for their inadequacy and also get attention and care. But their feelings of rejection perpetuates itself as the irritation of those who have to take care of them gradually expresses itself, and more intense self-hate manifests itself in additional physical symptoms.

Other escapes are attempting to win acceptance by bragging and lying, bullying others to get even, hatred of others, escape into the half-world of drugs or alcoholism, and delinquent or criminal behavior. The rejected child becomes an angry, unhappy adult, not because he is actually worthless, but because in his subconscious mind he thinks he is. He is endowed with the same equipment as others, and he is inadequate because he has been programmed to accept an untruth.

In cases of extreme anxiety and depression an Hypnotherapist should be consulted. He will regress the patient to the period of his life when the fear stimulus first became overintensified. While in hypnosis he gains emotional insight by observing the cause of the trauma from an adult viewpoint. Being exposed to the trauma while in a pleasantly relaxed state, he learns to accept it at face value rather than the childish exaggeration he had interpreted it to be.

Most feelings of mild anxiety and apprehension can be neutralized by the proper suggestions while in self-hypnosis. Self-crippling fear of criticism, fear of failure and fear of rejection can also be dealt with successfully. The chronic worrier can be helped. The following affirmation, when used with self-hypnosis twice daily, will give you self-confidence and overcome these self-defeating habits. It will make you a much happier and healthier person.

AFFIRMATION FOR ANXIETY

As you go deeper into a totally relaxed state, you are aware of a great transformation taking place in your personality. You are constantly growing and maturing, and realizing a new sense of self-confidence. You are aware of a new freedom. Your judgment is good, and you are fully capable of making the proper decisions. You like yourself and others like you. You do good things for yourself, and you enjoy doing good things for others. You believe in yourself more every day. You are learning to act boldly, because you are tapping the wisdom and energy of your subconscious mind. You are directing your life and you know life can bring the good things to you. You feel a warmth and friendship for the people you meet, and they return this warmth to you. You are sorry for those few who don't accept friendship easily, but you understand them and give a little extra to make them like you. Your smile and your friendly feelings draw them out of their self-centered attitudes, and they like you the more for your tolerance and understanding. You radiate confidence when meeting new people. You have perfect confidence that you can handle any situation you are confronted with. You are secure because you are confident. You deserve the best life has to offer, and you are tapping your inner resources to get the things you should have. You are poised, and you speak confidently, and with a steady strong voice. You are unique in that you are the only person exactly like YOU, and life has a good reason to express itself through your complex personality. You like people and people like you. They like you because you are confident and strong, and because you express yourself clearly. Each day you become more secure, and more capable of giving and receiving love. You are a happy, confident person, and you have a great respect for yourself. Other people are attracted to you, and give you their sincere friendship, and you deserve it. You are discovering many talents that are now emerging from your subconscious, and you are letting your imagination work for you. Every day you feel more confident that you can handle and solve any problem life has to offer, because you are a good, lovable person and you think clearly and act positively. You have poise, confidence and ability.

(If not recorded) All of the true concepts and affirmations are symbolized by the words "Self-confidence."

GIVING UP

This is usually a problem of older people but some develop it at middle age. Women who allow their children to be their whole reason for living sometimes suffer severe depressions when the last child moves out, and leaves them with "nothing to live for." Older people sometimes feel unwanted and uncared for, and lose interest in life. In effect, they give up.

Studies of animals show that when they are placed in life-threatening situations they tend to give up and die before their capacity for resistance is exhausted. Animals forced into a tank of water give up and drown long before they tire. Examinations of prey recovered before the dominant animal had a chance to devour it shows the death blow was never struck. These animals gave up, and the mere act of giving up caused their death.

Humans, too, die when they give up. Death does not come as swiftly, but it is nevertheless certain. John Shane, at the age of sixty-seven, was in good health and quite active for his age. He had managed a hardware store for many years and was gregarious and well-liked by his customers. The owner of the store sold out to a chain organization and they replaced Mr. Shane with a younger man. Although he was financially secure, he died in six months. During the first month he tried unsuccessfully to find another job, and then he gave up. He aged ten years in appearance in five months and died in his sleep soon thereafter. This is a very common example of death by abdication. Giving up is certain death. When it becomes impossible to continue with an established interest, another must be substituted. The suggestion that a bored person get a hobby falls on deaf ears, but when we by-pass the conscious mind and suggest it to the subconscious it is supplied with the interest and the energy necessary to keep the life-affirming forces working at full capacity.

Extreme boredom with life is often a forerunner of giving up. The bored person usually turns his thoughts inward, and interferes with the vital functions of the body in much the same manner as the person who tries to think of which foot to put forward while running downstairs. The results are disastrous in any case, although more immediate in the latter. Psychosomatic symptoms of illness are common, and the destructive forces can only be reversed by creating an interest in something other than the bodily functions.

Mrs. B., in her late fifties, who was suffering from extreme boredom with its psychosomatic results, was given a suggestion while in hypnosis that she wanted to build a doll house. She was told it was to be a three-story house standing at least three feet high with many rooms and windows. She would also make the miniature furniture for the house because that would be more of an accomplishment than buying it. The suggestion was chosen because she had read a magazine article about others who had made doll houses, and she was mildly interested. Her interest, though—like most of her others—stopped far short of any action. After repeating her self-hypnosis for a few days and getting through to her subconscious, she started drawing plans for her house, and within a week she was so interested in her project she forgot all about her aches and pains, heartburn and headaches. Although the house is incomplete after six months, her interest has not diminished in the least, and the tiny hand-carved stairway banisters and the intricate handmade furniture attest to the many pleasurable hours she has spent on her hobby. A bonus feature is the admiration of the people who come to see the house. Boredom has been replaced with interest and illness with vibrant health!

I cannot structure an example suggestion to fit all hobbies, and you will undoubtedly want to choose your own. But if you suffer from boredom or if you have lost interest in life, structure an affirmation according to the principles of suggestion outlined in Chapter Three. When used with self-hypnosis, it will place an interest in your chosen hobby or activity in your subconscious mind, which will furnish the energy and the desire to carry it out.

Chapter V

OTHER MIND EXPANDING PRACTICES

PRACTICES OF MYSTICISM

Many people prefer the mysterious to the scientific. They have faith in things they do not understand, and prefer to trust the unknown rather than any body of established facts. A useful and practical form of self-hypnosis is available to them with all the trappings of the mysterious. It is called meditation, and uses secret words and mysteries from the Far East. The principal difference between meditation and the hypnotic techniques of the Western world is one of religion. In what we call self-hypnosis, you may choose your own programming, be it self-actualization, better concentration, breaking of undesirable habits, or all of these and more. In meditation you are programmed by the concepts and philosophy of a Far Eastern culture.

An Overview Of Meditation, Bio-Feedback, Faith Healing And ESP

Many meditators feel the additional need to join a group or cult, with some type of father figure to hold in reverence. A great variety of religious groups offer ceremonies or practices that alter the state of consciousness. Those who don't need a holy man, and those who prefer to keep their own religious convictions, may avoid the influence of exotic philosophies as well as the initiation fees, by using one of the meditations described in this chapter.

These meditation groups are similar to the Western church denominations in that their adherents all claim the movement they have joined is the only true road to understanding, and their leader is the most enlightened. The hypnotic indoctrination of joy in working with the group leads many into a form of servitude. The mystic groups' use of meditation, whether it be the Sufi's graceful movements or the motionless concentration of TM, is reinforced by daily affirmation while in the trance state.

You can use meditation to induce the trance state without the indoctrination ceremonies of the cults, and choose your own reprogramming. And you only will choose the habits you eliminate or the self improvement you make. You may choose any of the following meditation techniques and enjoy the same trance state as self hypnosis. In fact, one of the self-hypnosis induction methods described in Chapter Two of this book utilizes the mantra type meditation described next. Meditation without philosophic programming still offers you complete relaxation and freedom from stress, with its resulting renewed energy, decreased anxiety and improved physical and psychological health.

THE MANTRA MEDITATION

Self hypnosis induced by the repetition of prayer or gods' names has long been a practice of Far Eastern religions. The mantra, meaning "man-mind" in Sanskrit, is a word or phrase that is repeated over and over by the meditator, until he drifts into an altered state of consciousness. Practically every mystical school teaches this procedure and it is one of the easiest to learn.

Begin by seating yourself comfortably in a chair and allow a couple of minutes to pass just thinking of nothing and getting relaxed. Then close your eyes and sit for another minute to allow your nervous system to calm down. Then start repeating your mantra, the word or phrase you have chosen. For this practice session, we will use the word 'One.' Repeat "one" over and over silently to yourself. Disregard all thoughts that try to invade your mind, and when they do, concentrate all the more on the mantra. You will soon reach an enjoyable relaxed state in which your awareness shifts inward. When you find yourself forgetting to repeat the mantra, start repeating it again. The first time you forget to repeat it you are

in a trance state, and your subconscious is open to suggestion.
Every time you become aware that you are not repeating the
mantra, start repeating it again, as long as you wish to stay in
hypnosis.

This is a very simple induction method, and if you have
recorded a suggestion, allow it to start playing back to you
when you are well into the trance state. This can be done by
leaving enough blank tape before your voice starts, to allow
you to turn the playback on before you start meditating.

There are various opinions as to what word or words to
use as a mantra. A word that has no meaning to you is best (in
my opinion) because the goal is to avoid thinking about
anything, and if you choose the word "Dog" you might
visualize a dog, and drift off into thinking about a dog you
once owned or a dog story. The word "One" was suggested by
Dr. Herbert Benson in his book *THE RELAXATION
RESPONSE*. "One" narrows things down a lot, and can be
repeated by most people without stimulating thought. "Om,"
pronounced "Ahm" is a universally used mantra meaning
"The infinite." "Hum" is also a Sanskrit word meaning "The
infinite within the finite." "Juana" in Sanskrit means "The
pure void, the function of which is intuitive wisdom."

Some meditators believe the mantra should have specific
content, such as "God is Love" or "All is one." Others, such
as the Transcendental Meditation teachers, believe that certain
sounds are better for certain people, and they are the only ones
who can tell (and sell) you a mantra. If they are right, all of the
other centuries-old mystical schools are wrong.

Choose a mantra, and if you don't get good results, try
another. Meditate for fifteen or twenty minutes twice daily.
Results vary with different people. If you are an average
person without too many hang-ups, you will get immediate
benefits. If you are quite neurotic, you may need a Guru to
comfort you and tell you to vary your rhythm of repetition or
to keep on truckin'.

You may come out of the trance angry, or depressed.
Your Guru will explain that this is not uncommon at first,

because as you release stress, trauma sometimes accompanies the process, and it is a matter of things getting slightly worse before they get a whole lot better. Sometimes your Guru will offer you a placebo by changing your mantra or suggesting a different rhythm for repeating it. He may also increase your faith by allowing you to go into a weekend retreat and meditate with a group. Then, as each meditator describes his experience, you find that your own is not unique, and you are also encouraged by those who are enthusiastic and pleased with the results.

Granting that you are near normal and of average intelligence, you can learn meditation without a teacher by a few trial and error practice runs.

TRANSCENDENTAL MEDITATION

Transcendental meditation, or TM as it is usually called, is the mantra meditation technique just described, with one exception. You agree to keep your mantra a secret, and only the Guru leader or one of his approved teachers can give it to you. (There is an old saying among the various teachers of mysticism that anyone who tries to sell you a mantra is pulling your leg.)

Most mystical philosophies demand a rigid life style of diet, ritual and exercise, which is either impractical or too severe for the average person who is busy making a living. The idea of a practical meditation practice for the poor workers originated in the mind of one of the four most prominent religious leaders in India, Swami Brahamananda Saraswati, also called Guru Dev. When approaching death he called his favorite disciple to his side and gave him a sacred assignment. He asked him to formulate a simple meditation and teach it to the poor of India, a project he himself had hoped to carry out during his lifetime, but had neglected because of the many duties of his high office. This favorite disciple and pupil of Guru Dev was called Mahesh Prasad Varma, later to become the Maharishi Mahesh Yogi. The great teacher's hope was to bring greater peace and tranquillity to the poor of India.

Mahesh secluded himself in the Himalaya Mountains for two years and emerged with the common mantra meditation without the usual restrictions and disciplines. He called his method Transcendental Meditation, and declared it superior to all other mystical practices, as most Gurus are inclined to do. He further declared that only he, or one he had trained, could give students their secret word, or mantra. Different people, he explained, needed different mantras because of different rhythms in the various organs of their bodies.

After working with the common people of India for a while, he grew restless because of his slow progress, and traveled to England. There he established the International Meditation Society in London, where the Beatles brought him international publicity with their support. The Maharishi, however, demanded a different type of support from the Beatles, in the form of a large sum of money, and this caused them to reject him publicly as too materialistic.

The Maharishi then traveled to the United States, where he became somewhat of a celebrity by appearing on numerous TV talk shows. Here he established the Students' Meditation Society, and it was decided to reserve all TM instruction for those who could afford a fee, which at this writing is one hundred and twenty-five dollars for adults, and seventy-five dollars for students.

Since all TM students are required to keep their mantra secret and also required not to teach anyone else the procedure, it is impossible for anyone to practice TM technically without paying their required fee. However, you will be practicing the same meditation procedure as TM without the secret word by using the mantra meditation described earlier. Recent experiments with mantras picked at random prove they get the same results as TM, the results varying with the type of improvement the meditator is indoctrinated to expect. Dr. Herbert Benson and Dr. Robert

Keith Wallace, both of the Harvard Medical School, did extensive research on the psychological correlates of TM, and their findings were reported in numerous articles in scientific journals. Dr. Benson asserts that anyone may apply the principles of TM without spending money for a secret mantra.

The TM indoctrination consists of two lectures in which the benefits are explained and documented, with testimonials and scientific data. Those who pay the initiation fee usually feel that they need help, and that TM will help them. This is one advantage of TM over a do-it-yourself system. Since hypnosis is a conviction phenomenon, expectation is necessary to results, and the degree of results depends upon faith in the outcome. The lectures are very convincing, and you go into the first trance at the initiation ceremony with heightened expectation amid solemn surroundings.

The initiation is conducted in a small room which is bare except for a table and two chairs. On the table is a lighted candle, some burning incense, and a picture of the Guru Dev. You are required to bring some flowers, a white handkerchief and some fruit. Your teacher places these articles in a basket, sets them on the table in front of the Guru's picture, and chants praises in Sanskrit of the Guru and others before him. Then he tells you your secret word, or mantra, and has you repeat it a number of times, checking you carefully on the pronunciation.

You are then asked to sit silently and repeat your secret word over and over until you go into the typical trance state of meditation. This state of self-hypnosis immediately following the instructions to keep your mantra a secret results in subconscious acceptance of the suggestion, and the new meditator will find it very difficult to divulge the secret even though he might have a conscious desire to do so. He thinks he can do it, but in all probability he won't.

Meditation is one of the world's oldest spiritual disciplines, and the Far Eastern Holy Men believe enlightenment comes from within your own consciousness which is merged with the Cosmos. Therefore, your new knowledge and enlightenment through meditation comes from the all-knowing creator, creative intelligence, or what Christians consider God. Each Guru claims to have reached this state of God consciousness, and is therefore a superior being. The Maharishi has discovered "Prana" as a basic force of mind, which in the Yogic theory is Ch'i, the non-physical cosmic energy that created the universe.

Fundamental Christian groups, who opposed TM's becoming a required course in the Sacramento, California, public schools, blocked it by translating the initiation chants which praised past Hindu Holy men. They claimed "foreign gods" were being invoked, thereby violating the laws of separation of Church and State.

All meditation, including TM, is indeed a form of religious practice, the Far Eastern philosophy of Prana being a part and parcel of the concept. The laws of suggestion, mental expectancy and subconscious conviction by trance induction are inherent in the various disciplines. The Maharishi also claims that TM has nothing to do with hypnosis, but it involves going into a self-imposed trance, a state of heightened suggestibility in which the expected results suggested in the indoctrination lectures are internalized, and the modification of behavior. This is hypnotism.

A word to people who are already practicing TM. No other mantra than the one you have been given will work as well, because you are now conditioned to it by repeated concentrated exposure. New meditators will also do best by choosing a mantra, if necessary by trial and error, and then sticking to it. Meditate for fifteen or twenty minutes twice daily for best results.

THE MEDITATION OF THE BUBBLE

As in all non-movement meditation, first sit quietly without movement for a minute or two to relax your nervous system as much as possible. Then imagine you are sitting at the bottom of a lake. It is a quiet clear lake and you are able to breathe comfortably. Let your mind go blank and think of nothing as long as possible. When a thought finally insists upon coming into your mind, imagine a large bubble is starting to rise from the floor of the lake and slowly moving upward toward the surface. Watch the bubble rise. It takes six or seven seconds before it disappears through the surface of the water. Regard the thought as a bubble, and allow it to stay in your mind until the bubble rises and disappears. Then put it out of your mind. When another thought enters your mind, regard it, too, as a bubble, and allow your mind to harbor the thought for approximately seven seconds as the new bubble rises to the surface.

If the same thought occurs repeatedly, this is O.K. Each time it repeats, allow a new bubble to rise to the surface and then put it out of your mind. If you don't have any thoughts that is fine too. Just watch bubbles rise, each one taking approximately six or seven seconds. Possibly you will get a perception or a feeling rather than a thought. Feel, or perceive, for the few seconds necessary for the bubble to rise. It is important that you do not associate or compare the bubbles. Just learn to contemplate each thought or perception individually for this limited amount of time, and watch the bubble rise as you do. Then let go and put it out of your mind.

In this discipline you are meditating on the stream of your consciousness. Try this for ten minutes daily and see if it is a satisfactory method for you. If so, increase to twenty minutes daily after a week or two.

BREATH COUNTING

The object of this meditation is to discipline yourself to do and think one thing as completely as possible. You sit or lie in a comfortable position and count each exhaled breath. Think "One" as you exhale. Think "and" as you inhale, and then think "Two" as you exhale again, and so on in units of seven. After you have counted seven exhalations, go back to one again. You may find it easier to count in units of four or five. In Zen training they use units of ten, and this is permissible unless you have difficulty remembering which number you counted last. The object is to keep your entire concentration on the counting to the exclusion of everything else. Do not stray away from the discipline by modifying your breathing or accepting any other thoughts, feelings or sensory perceptions. You may close your eyes or leave them open. If you close them, it is permissible to peek at a clock occasionally so that you will know how long you are meditating. Fifteen minutes is a good timing for beginners, and the period may be increased, as you get more adept.

CONTEMPLATION

This is called One pointing in the Eastern mystical schools. The object is to pick an object such as a seashell, a leaf, or any other small object that is interesting to you, and to look at it so intently you "feel it" with your eyes. Look at it so alertly, and actively, you are binding your mind to it, seeing it in your mind's eye rather than with your sense organs. When anything other than the contemplated object comes into your mind, put it aside and go back to the discipline. Do not strain your eyes by staring at the object, but relax them while keeping it in view. It is your mind that should be exploring and perceiving the object, and your eyes are necessary only for transmission.

Once you have decided upon an object of contemplation, stay with it for at least two weeks. This meditation will go quite differently at different sessions. You should become totally involved in looking and feeling. You may feel more relaxed if your object of contemplation is sitting on a table in front of you, so you may hold it in your hand and bring it closer to your eyes at times. Fifteen minute periods are recommended for the first two weeks, and if you wish to stay with this discipline you may wish to increase the time to half an hour daily.

THE "SAFE HARBOR" MEDITATION

Rather than a discipline, this meditation is a drifting and dreaming experience. As you close your eyes, imagine you are adrift in your own consciousness. There is turbulence elsewhere, but you are in a calm place, and you feel as though you are seeking some spot where you will feel perfectly peaceful and secure. You feel that you have been there before, but don't know what or where the place is. You sense a signal of some kind drawing you to this place. You make no effort, but you allow yourself to be drawn to this place, or way of being, which is your own safe harbor. There you will be perfectly "at home." You may drift for a while but eventually you find your own safe harbor, and it will be a place where you can go when you want perfect peace and contentment. After resting for a while, you will be able to come out and face the world with renewed energy and confidence. I cannot describe your safe harbor, for it won't be like anyone else's. But you will know when you find it. This is a very pleasant meditation, and should be practiced for fifteen or twenty minutes daily. You can close your eyes at any time, and let your mind drift to your safe harbor. There you will find peace and contentment, and refuge from the stress of everyday living.

A GROUP MEDITATION WITH MOTION

This is a Sufi type meditation, and it requires a group of from five to twenty people. You form a circle and clasp hands, standing about two feet apart. Slowly lean backward and face the sky while bringing your arms upwards, and yell "Ya Hai." Then lean forward and bring the arms down and backward until you are facing the ground, and yell "Ya Huk." Then repeat the procedure over and over in a rhythm that is comfortable for the group. The "Ya Hai" sound is sustained slightly, and the "Ya Huk" sound ends abruptly. The goal is to get your second wind by going past the fatigue point. If any one of the group feels that he should not continue beyond a certain point he may step back and place the hands of the people on either side of him together.

This exercise integrates body and mind awareness. The group in motion resembles the opening and closing of a flower, the flower being a particular object of reverence in Far Eastern religions.

Annoying the neighbors and disturbing the peace should not be the goal or by-product of any religion, however, and this exercise should be practiced only in places where it is appropriate.

BIOFEEDBACK

Biofeedback was pioneered by the Menninger Clinic in Topeka, Kansas. It has been used successfully in many other research centers throughout the world. It is a technique that teaches patients to consciously control bodily functions which are normally controlled by the subconscious mind. It has proved useful in controlling symptoms of psychosomatic diseases such as asthma, skin eruptions, migraine headaches, peptic ulcers and chronic pain.

Sensors are used to monitor the patient's skin temperature, brain function and nerve action. These signals are amplified and shown on a dial for the patient to observe. He attempts to change the dial reading by concentration. As he discovers his mind can truly control his body, he feels a new awareness and confidence, and can watch himself alter his bodily functions by reading the dial. He finds that he is no longer entirely controlled by exterior forces, and thus learns to minimize the stress reaction. Since stress is often the cause of psychosomatic disorders, the symptoms are soon eliminated and the chance of their return is minimized. When the patient learns to control the bodily functions that respond unfavorably to stress without observing the dial he is better able to cope with the problems of daily living.

Biofeedback requires highly sophisticated and expensive equipment, and a number of visits to a doctor who is trained in the technique. People who can afford it, and who prefer professional help to a do-it-yourself routine will find it very helpful. Self-Hypnosis, however, is a much more simple and complete method of gaining control of the subconscious, and offers you many more self-improvement opportunities when used with properly constructed suggestions.

WITCHCRAFT, VOODOO AND BLACK MAGIC

Dr. Harry Abram, professor of psychiatry at the Vanderbilt University of Nashville, Tennessee, described a patient who was lying critically ill in a hospital, slowly dying because of a death wish placed on her by her mother-in-law. The doctors could find nothing physically wrong with the woman but she was convinced she would die, and her conviction was being realized. Dr. Abram fortunately understood the workings of black magic and witchcraft. He knew the woman would recover if she could be convinced that the hex had been removed. He had someone read a few verses from the Bible to her, and then told her the curse had been lifted and that she would recover. She was soon well.

Voodoo, black magic and witchcraft exert their influence by the aid of auto-suggestion. They work on the same principle as psychomatic disease and psychosomatic cure. A witch doctor can cure one who believes in witchcraft more surely than a medical doctor because his placebo is more believable. To his patient, a brew consisting of a pinch of powdered owl intestine, a secret quantity of black cat saliva, and two frog brains boiled in calf's blood and lard is much more powerful than a pill.

Lifting curses, drawing out devils, nixing hexes or faith healing by laying on of hands are all appropriate to the religion you have faith in. It is interesting to observe that the more primitive the religion or superstition, the more certain the cure, where psychosomatic illness is indicated. The subject usually has deeper conviction and greater expectation. So as long as people believe in charms, curses, witches' brew and mojos, the witch doctor will be a necessary part of society.

FAITH HEALING

Although faith healing has long been associated with religion, it has now emerged as a reliable practice without religious wrappings. Success in regression of cancerous tissues and disappearance of calcium overlay in cases of arthritis have been affirmed by many scientific observers, and increased speed in the healing of wounds is well-established.

Recently one of the world's largest pharmaceutical firms offered a series of tapes dealing with the results of faith healing research, and twenty-seven thousand doctors and psychiatrists requested and received them. This illustrates how many doctors are aware of the amazing potential of faith healing techniques.

That the body is a complete laboratory in itself has long been realized, but since the subconscious controls the medication, it often not only withholds the cure but causes the disease by disrupting the bodily functions it is supposed to supervise and coordinate. "What is expected tends to be realized" is a law of mind that can cause disease or cure it. The conscious mind determines how the subconscious energy is applied by the thoughts it holds and the emotions it entertains. Faith healing might be called natural healing, because it utilizes the body's own resources. It has long been known that when dangerous bacteria invade the body, millions of white blood corpuscles are manufactured in the bone marrow and rushed to the affected parts to engage the intruders and kill them. If you could watch these amazing wars that take place in your blood stream, you would see a parallel of our larger world with navies at war. A white corpuscle approaches a disease germ in much the same manner as a warship closes in on an enemy vessel. Through a microscope you can watch it part and half surround the germ cell, and actually attack it with what appears to be bombs and shells. Tiny explosions are plainly seen, and soon the germ disintegrates. Researchers at Baylor College of Medicine recently discovered a substance they call Antineoplastons in the human body that kills five types of cancer without harming normal cells. They are considered to be the body's natural defense against cancer, and when they are inhibited in their normal functioning, cancer may result. The spontaneous remission which occurs once in thousands of cancer cases must be the result of the body's ability to correct this condition, and effect a normal release of this cancer-controlling substance. How else can cases of terminally ill cancer patients being kept alive by faith healers be explained? There are many such well documented cases, and these healers are certainly not magicians.

An English faith healer is astonishing doctors by keeping a number of terminally ill cancer patients alive and free of pain for years after they were expected to die. Medical doctors of statute attest to the complete absence of cancer in patients they had given six months to live. The healer, Gilbert Anderson, uses a non-religious approach. The patients are first taught a meditation relaxing technique combined with breathing exercises. While in the self-imposed state of hypnosis they are taught to imagine what the cancer growth in their bodies looks like, and imagine healthy cells attacking and killing it. The healer also did the "laying on of hands" act on the areas that were diseased, and the patients' condition improved.

Dr. Ainslee Meares, an Australian psychiatrist, taught a women who was dying of cancer a form of self-hypnosis to re-establish the body's own immunological defenses. She had been treated with surgery and radiation without lasting results, and was weakening daily. Dr. Nigel Gray, director of the Anti-Cancer Council of Victoria, confirmed that she was dying when she went to Dr. Meares, but that she had gone into a real remission after his meditation treatments. Dr. John M. Bradley, head of the Peter MacCallum Cancer Institute in Melbourne at whose clinic she was treated before she went to Dr. Meares, agreed that Dr. Meares had helped her improve her condition perceptibly, and that he had no medical explanation for it. This was not a faith healing case, but the treatment and results point up the fact that the body and mind, when properly synchronized, have a defense system which has been largely neglected in today's treatment of disease.

If you value your life, don't let anything I have said in this discourse on faith healing keep you from a good medical doctor when you are ill. Often a virus infection or a bacterial invasion can kill you before your body can muster enough defense to defeat it. Faith healing is not yet an exact science and sometimes it works for one person and not for another. Christ said, "Be of good comfort, thy faith hath made thee whole," acknowledging that faith, not He, had cured a man who had been sick on his back for twelve years. But He added that He was without honor in his home town and could work no miracles there. Any good doctor can save you if you catch a cancer in time, and you are playing Russian roulette if you delay seeing one. Faith healing should only be used as an adjunct to medical or surgical treatment, until there is more research on the subject.

The miracles of Lourdes are good examples of faith cures. Pomponatius remarked that if the bones of an animal were substituted for the bones of a saint, the cures attributed to them would be just as effective so long as the patient was unaware of the change. Any religious conviction is a subconscious conviction and faith is another word for both.

Researchers have also recently discovered a substance which, when secreted by the human brain, acts much like morphine to kill pain. These known immunizing and pain controlling substances, and perhaps many other undiscovered secretions at the disposal of the subconscious, are perhaps responsible for the faith healings we presently consider miraculous. More research is definitely indicated.

EXTRA SENSORY PERCEPTION

In studying the complexities of the mind, science is attempting to study the force that created it. Our sense organs reveal only a small portion of the living universe to us, and our knowledge of it is therefore limited. Insects will gather on ultra-violet rays humans cannot see. Dogs answer to high-pitched whistles humans cannot hear. Humans perceive infra-red heat waves by touch which they cannot visualize. There are probably many things happening in the space and time about us we will never be able to perceive with our limited sensory capacity, and many things we do perceive will be incomprehensible to us.

Man, like nature, abhors a vacuum. Events beyond the scope of his present understanding are treated in a way that makes him the most comfortable. Take, for example, the flying saucers, which have become a common source of frustration because of continued reported sightings. A great many people make themselves mentally comfortable by denying they exist, and labeling the people who sighted them crackpots or publicity seekers. Others are certain they are from another planet. Very few, however, admit that the facts are not all in yet, and regard the present evidence as inconclusive. John Dewey said, in effect, that the intelligent person who uses his mind correctly is capable of holding judgment in suspension until all of the facts relative to the situation are known.

John Dewey's concept of correct thinking applies perfectly to many aspects of extra-sensory perception, or ESP. Scientists and the lay public alike seem to either scoff at the possibility of such nonsense, or enthusiastically embrace it as a scientifically proven fact. Neither is entirely correct. Many thousands of events which are unexplainable within the limits of our sensory perceptions have been reported and witnessed to by people of unquestionable integrity. But this is not scientific proof by controlled experiment. The results of laboratory experiments have been, and probably always will be, disappointing, because in most cases these occurrences are not directed by the will. They are limited by the fact that a great emotional need is necessary for the phenomena to take place, and there must be a strong emotional tie between the two people participating.

Experiments at Duke University have shown that one phase of extra-sensory perception, that of mental telepathy, can be studied in the laboratory. This one aspect of ESP is subject to the will. Dr. J. L. Rhine employed card guessing techniques in which he used packs of "Zener" cards. Each pack consisted of five sets of five cards each, bearing five patterns; a circle, a star, three wavy lines, a cross and a square. The subjects guessed which card was turned up when cards were picked at random from a shuffled pack. There were twenty-five cards so the law of probability would suggest five correct picks for each run of twenty-five. After thousands of guesses, the students tested averaged scores of more than two to one over those attributed to chance, and some students beat the odds by over two million to one.

Many in the scientific community didn't take kindly to Dr. Rhine's announcements of success, and attributed it to an unusual run of luck. Any professional gambler knows he can hold good poker hands night after night, for hours of play, and that he can also get a streak of bad hands that defy all the laws of probability. So other scientists duplicated his experiments, taking even greater precautions against error or cheating. Some found their results explainable by the laws of chance, while others discovered a displacement effect in the guesses. The card drawn previous to the one turned up and the next card to be drawn was often guessed out of all proportion to the laws of chance. Certain subjects showed an ability to guess future cards, which neither he nor the experimenter knew, or the last card drawn which only the experimenter knew, against a million to one odds. However, they couldn't duplicate their successful guessing at every sitting, so others were unconvinced.

Aside from the great mass of people who only believe what they want to believe, there is logical reasoning behind skepticism and conviction alike. The logical skeptic attributes all things that defy scientific explanation to coincidence or falsehood. The logical believer is usually one with first-hand ESP experience, or one who knows and trusts someone who has it. The scientific method was set up to judge facts which can be revealed by the five senses. Since the mind seems to encompass more than our present limited senses can perceive, it can probably never understand itself fully by the scientific method.

There are some strange phenomena that science cannot explain away by coincidence or trickery, and many find it more comfortable to put them out of their minds. By not accepting the incident, they are not troubled by any desire to solve it. The "Bah-humbug" group have little to say when confronted by the puzzling talents of Peter Hurkos or Gerald Croiset. Croiset has made himself available for serious experimentation for years, and has repeatedly described the person who would occupy a certain theatre seat, picked at random by the experimenter, in minute detail. Hurkos is famous for his work with law enforcement agencies, and has solved many murder cases by a power he himself does not understand. He helped the Limburg police solve the murder of a young miner by holding the victim's coat. After a few minutes he felt that the murderer was the young man's stepfather, whom he described as a man who wore glasses and had a wooden leg. He also told the police the motive: the murderer loved the miner's wife. He gave the police the location of the murder weapon, a gun which they found on the roof of the victim's house. One such incident might be suspect as an elaborate conspiracy between Hurkos and the entire Limburg police force to fool the public (which is almost ludicrous thinking) but that would not explain the many other police department's successes with Hurkos, and their careful checks of his honesty. He has, in fact, solved many crimes by an uncanny sense no one yet understands. This may not be ESP, but what is it?

On the skeptic's side, an interesting question is often asked. If Hurkos, Croiset or other so-called Psychics could ferret out a criminal for the police or do the many other feats attributed to them, why don't they make a fortune at the races? The answer is usually that they only use this great power to help others. This is hard to accept as anything but a ludicrous evasion. These people are human, and have needs like all of us. If they actually are saints in human clothing, they would do well to collect from the race track and feed the hungry. It would be more probable, though, that they are limited in their capabilities. Hurkos may be able to hold a garment belonging to someone he doesn't know and "see" things about them, but he may not be able to hold a horse's hoof or saddle and tell how fast he will run today!

Skepticism is perpetuated by those who are too lazy to accomplish much in life, and lay claim to being psychic as a means of being "somebody." But aside from the trickery, the lies, the schemes and the desire to believe, there are many genuine cases of what seems to be extra-sensory perception that we have not been able to explain away.

One theory states that we have an undeveloped sixth sense, which, in a very few people, is active to a certain degree. A more universally accepted theory among scientists who have given ESP serious study is that of universal or cosmic consciousness. This theory states that all intelligence is one, just as all matter is one. Scientists now know that all matter is condensed energy, and matter can be disposed of, as in the nuclear reaction, by releasing it as energy. If mind is capable of releasing matter, mind is capable of creating matter from energy. According to this theory, some type of mind created matter from energy, and various religions have various opinions as to what this First Cause, Spirit, or God is like.

Since matter is inert and has no power to move itself, it must be acted upon by some form of energy outside itself. The intelligence that creates matter from energy and that can reduce matter to energy, is universal intelligence, and we all share it. When man thinks, he thinks with a small segment of the One Mind of the universe. His mind is a part of one universal mind, although his conscious mind has a feeling of being an individual. Deep in the subconscious, all individuals are capable of drawing upon the knowledge of universal mind if they develop certain trance state techniques. The universal mind knows how every successful business was built and how every fortune was won. It knows how to build the exact structures of your vital organs, and how to keep them operating smoothly. It has universal knowledge. By this theory, what seems to be extra-sensory perception is understandable as communication with the innermost regions of the subconscious, which is said to have a connection with the universal mind. Extra-sensory perception is possible for anyone who develops the ability to go deeply enough into their subconscious.

Self-hypnosis is a means of contacting the subconscious mind, and the talented people who draw their creations from their subconscious may be tapping universal consciousness without consciously understanding the process. The power of the subconscious is awe-inspiring. Health, wealth, and probably other things yet undreamed of are possible if we learn to tap its knowledge and energy. So if you get better acquainted with your own subconscious mind, you may have some ESP experiences that will benefit you beyond all expectations.

PRE-BIRTH REGRESSION

By hypnotizing a subject we can regress him to his early childhood years, and his speech and demeanor are those of a child. We can also go further, and regress him past the date of his birth to what appears to be a series of other lives. The subject may speak in a foreign language he has not learned in his present life, and in the dialect of the period he is regressed to. Could this be evidence of re-incarnation? Many believe it is.

Another explanation is that the subject is tapping Universal Consciousness, which is said to be available to the subconscious mind under certain trance conditions. If this is true, he is momentarily reliving another life that someone else lived.

Re-incarnation, like other spiritual beliefs, must be accepted on faith. So, also, must Universal Consciousness. Whether or not you are reliving your own or someone else's previous life when regressed through hypnotism, or whether there is some other explanation which is not conceivable with our present knowledge, is open for further investigation. The evidence of re-incarnation is impressive though not conclusive, and I am certain some of my readers will want to explore it further. You can't help being impressed when you hear a subject describe his or her life style in some far-away country, and then vividly describe his own death and his feelings as he views his body after leaving it. You may be curious enough to allow a qualified hypnotist to take you back to a former life, and to discover when and who you were before your present experience on this earth. Your "roots" may go further back than you may believe!

Chapter VI

WEALTH, EDUCATION AND WELFARE THROUGH SELF HYPNOSIS

RELIEF OF PSYCHOSOMATIC SYMPTOMS

Some doctors classify psychosomatic diseases as those which have no seeming physical cause. An example is a woman who complains of a persistant pain in her chest. Tests and X-rays prove nothing to be wrong in that area of her body, but the pain persists. Many doctors, including psychiatrists, now are using a more broad definition of the term psychosomatic, and include diseases that are physical in nature, but originate in the mental processes. Many even suspect that the mental state of a patient determines whether he will accept or repel a bacterial invasion.

Every thought has a physical response, and every act has its emotional counterparts. As long as you live, your body and mind are one. The passive observation of a tree or a flower sets

Expansion Of Your Abilities To Become Healthy, Wealthy And Wise

in motion a physical response involving millions of nerve cells from the retina of the eye to the various parts of the brain. The very thought of a tree produces similar activity that can involve millions of brain cells comparing associated memories. This is physical activity. All mental activity depends upon physical changes in the tissues of the body.

Your mind can make you sick, and conversely, your mind can make you well. This does not mean the trouble is all in your mind. The pain and symptoms are real. But the trouble started in your mind, and it can be treated by redirecting your mind.

To better understand the affirmations that follow, it would be helpful to review the first several pages of chapter four, which explain how disruptive emotions disturb the delicate chemical balance of the body. Symptoms can be eliminated by reversing the process through auto suggestion while in self hypnosis.

Repetition and emphasis are necessary to warn you not to treat symptoms without first consulting a doctor. Pain or other symptoms may be a warning of serious disorders that can only be treated successfully by emergency measures. Certain drugs work faster than the mechanisms of the body, for both mind and body must have time to reverse their course to effect a cure. The cancer patients described in the last chapter, who had been kept alive, and in some cases cured by mental processes, had all received full medical and surgical treatment before using hypnosis as a therapy.

Auto suggestion, used properly with hypnosis, in conjunction with medical help, will speed recovery and alleviate pain and discomfort. If the doctor diagnoses the disease as psychosomatic, hypnosis is the best cure.

Gil Boyne, called the hypnotist of the stars because of his work with many of Hollywood's leading performers, tells of a case of a terminally ill cancer patient who was referred to him by a leading doctor. The doctor estimated he had only about six months to live, and asked Mr. Boyne to relieve his pain by hypnosis. First he was taught self-hypnosis, and then glove anesthesia, described later in this chapter. Mr. Boyne has received Christmas cards from the patient for three years now, and it seems he is still doing well. Whether the relief of pain or the change of attitude toward it slowed the progress of the disease is not known, but the patient is certainly ahead of the game, and free of pain, as a result of learning self hypnosis.

HEADACHE

Where the cause is not physical pathology, headaches can be treated successfully by suggestions for general relaxation. The following affirmation, when used with self-hypnosis, will be successful in alleviating the pain, even in cases as severe as migraine.

"Now that you are completely relaxed, and in a deep hypnotic sleep, let go, all over, once again. Soooo relaxed. Soooo lazy. Now all the muscles in your forehead are letting go. They are getting looser-looser-relaxed and limp. This loose, relaxed feeling spreads to your eyes—Your eyes are so relaxed—so comfortable. Your forehead is loose and all the muscles are relaxed and limp. Your eyes are loose and relaxed. The loose feeling goes over the top of your head and your whole scalp is relaxed. You feel better and better. Now all the muscles in the neck let go—all loose and limp—relaxed and comfortable. The base of your skull is all loose and relaxed. You feel so good! Better and better. You feel much better, relaxing more and more. Your neck muscles are now completely relaxed and comfortable. Your whole head is relaxed and comfortable. You feel wonderful! Your head and neck feel clear. You feel good. You feel absolutely wonderful! All the muscles and nerves in your head and neck are completely relaxed and you feel fine. When you awaken you will continue to feel fine. You will feel better and better for the rest of the day. You feel absolutely perfect! All of your neck and head muscles and nerves are completely relaxed." Use the usual awakening procedure, and follow the instructions in chapter three. If your headache isn't entirely gone when you come back to conscious awareness, it will gradually disappear within fifteen or twenty minutes.

CONSTIPATION

Constipation can be relieved whether or not the problem is of psychosomatic origin. Use the following affirmation for a week or two and you will get dramatic results.

"Now, as you go deeper and deeper into a comfortable, hypnotic sleep, your lips are beginning to relax. As they become loose and limp, your jaws also relax, and your teeth separate so they do not quite touch. The wave of relaxation spreads down your esophagus,—down, down, down to your stomach. As you go deeper, your whole gastro-intestinal system relaxes. Your gastro intestinal system is merely a long tube equipped with muscles that relax and contract alternately. When you relax your mouth and throat, a chain reaction starts, down through your esophagus, on through your stomach and duodenum, down through the small and large intestines to the rectum. The rectum signals when it is full, and you feel the urge to empty it. These muscles always work perfectly because they are relaxed. Every time you start a meal you start a natural process of relaxation. When you chew and swallow food, the alternate waves of relaxation and contraction starts, and continue on down through your esophagus and stomach, and through your intestines all the way down through the colon to your rectum. When you eat, you start a natural and easy process by relaxing your gastro-intestinal track and allowing it to proceed toward a process of natural elimination. Soon after each meal you have an urge to move your bowels. You always go to the toilet immediately when you get this urge. When you sit on the toilet seat, the contact of your flesh with seat will be a signal to your subconscious mind. It will be a signal to empty the rectum. You know your gastro-intestinal system is only a long tube which winds about in your body. When you eat, you start a chain reaction of muscles which surround this long tube. They alternately relax and contract, all the way from your throat to your rectum, where the waste is deposited. You get an urge to go to the toilet soon after eating, and you always go to the toilet when you get this urge. The first bite of food starts the muscles relaxing, then contracting, then relaxing, and then contracting, until your food passes through the long tube and enters your rectum. When your rectum is full you get the urge to go to the toilet. When you sit down on the seat it is a signal to empty your rectum. Your rectum empties itself without conscious effort.

Use this affirmation with self hypnosis twice daily until a natural habit is established. Try not to think about the contents of the affirmation while eating, or while on the toilet. This is a subconscious process and conscious effort will impede it.

RELIEF OF PAIN

The threshold of pain can be raised in direct proportion to the relaxation of the muscles. Since anxiety leads to tenseness, it intensifies pain. However, it has been proved that fear cannot be experienced when the body is completely relaxed. So hypnosis banishes fear and raises the pain threshold automatically. Hypnotize yourself and imagine your left hand is emersed in a pail of ice water, with salt added to make it colder. Imagine your right hand is emersed in a bucket of hot water. Your left hand becomes numb with the cold. You are aware of the comfort and warmth of your right hand. Your left hand becomes completely numb, like a block of wood. Alternate feeling the numbness of the left hand and the heightened feeling of heat on the right hand. You will be able to stick a needle in the left hand and not feel it.

Just imagining a portion of your body to be numb, like a piece of wood, will deepen hypnosis and bring relief of pain.

When structuring your suggestions for relief of pain, keep in mind that the subconscious believes anything it is told. And it controls the mechanism that carries the pain signals to the brain. It also controls the production of white corpuscles and their transportation to effected areas. It can therefore not only alleviate pain, but eliminate the cause of the pain as well. The following suggestions need to be elaborated upon and repeated, but they carry the substance of the affirmation necessary for the general relief of both symptom and disease.

SUGGESTION FOR RELIEF OF
THE PAIN OF ARTHRITIS

"Arthritis is caused by deposits of calcium between the bones at the joints. Now, with each movement you make, a drop of lubricant is secreted. This natural lubricant covers the calcium and allows your joints to move in comfort. At the same time, the lubricant is dissolving the calcium, and your condition is improving daily. Your joints move in comfort because they are being lubricated. The calcium is gradually dissolving and you are feeling better every day," etc.

RELIEF OF BURSITIS PAIN

"Each time you move your arm, a drop of lubricant is released which will make you much more comfortable. Each time you move your arm you are getting better and more unaware of it. You will notice an improvement every day.

RELIEF OF PAIN BY INTERNAL AWARENESS

The fact that we can disrupt the activity of the subconscious mind by conscious interference works both ways. By consciously trying to go to sleep we can inhibit the natural process, because it is the function of the subconscious. But when the subconscious is engaged in an activity detrimental to our welfare, we can, in certain cases, consciously defeat its purpose. This is especially true of pain arising from muscular tension, and therefore applies to most head, neck and shoulder aches.

Let's assume you have a headache and you want to relieve the pain. Sit in a comfortable position. Concentrate on the pain. Feel it ache. Continue to think only of the ache, the way it feels, for several minutes. It will probably ache worse, but don't give up. Feel the pain, and exclude any other thoughts that come into your mind. You will be interfering with your subconscious, which is causing the tension. After five to eight minutes your pain will disappear.

Sometimes, after the headache goes, you will feel pain in your neck or shoulders. This is because your neck or shoulders ached before, but the dominant pain in your head took your attention. Use the same procedure with the neck or shoulders that you did with your head. This method is a form of self hypnosis, induced by concentrating on the sources of the pain, and it causes the muscles and nerve centers concentrated upon to relax, thereby eliminating the pain.

ASTHMA

Asthma is often triggered by allergy of some sort, but it is basically a symptom of suppressed anger. Asthma sufferers should review the portion of chapter four devoted to anger, and use the accompanying affirmation for relief or anger; because relief of anger is relief of asthma. A certain amount of mental trauma may be experienced, because as the stress of anger is released it will often be felt. Asthma sufferers often complain that when they come out of hypnosis they feel angry for no explainable reason, but this must be compared to the pain of pulling an aching tooth. It hurts, but it feels good after it has been pulled. Hypnotize yourself and use the affirmation for relief of anger twice daily, adding the following few lines at several intervals: "The muscles surrounding your bronchial tubes remain relaxed at all times. Relaxed when you inhale, relaxed when you exhale. Your bronchial tubes and the muscles that surround them are relaxed and normal. They remain relaxed and normal at all times. Your subconscious mind controls the muscles and nerves, and it keeps the bronchial tubes relaxed and the muscles that surround the bronchial tubes relaxed and normal. You breathe easily and normally at all times because these muscles are relaxed and normal."

QUICK RECOVERY FROM DISEASE

When used with conventional medical care, self hypnosis can speed recovery from any illness. Even terminal cancer patients surprise doctors by leading normal, pain free lives for years by this method. You can structure your own affirmation to suit your individual needs, but following is an example of the substance of the necessary suggestions.

"My body manufactures healthy cells that fight and kill harmful germs and bacteria. My body is manufacturing great quantities of these disease fighting cells and my arteries are transporting them to the areas where they are needed. These healthy cells are killing the invaders and I am getting better every hour—feeling better every hour."

This is the skeleton of the affirmation, and must be repeated and enlarged upon. If, for instance, you have an infected leg, think of the infected area, think of how it looks. Then visualize the antibodies destroying the germs, and replacing the diseased area with healthy flesh. This affirmation and visualization used properly with self hypnosis twice daily will bring about dramatic results!

MEMORY IMPROVEMENT

Minute changes occur in the cells of the nervous system as a result of every sensation or thought we experience. These changes are limitless because of the millions of interconnecting nerve cells, and they apparently affect numerous cells to form patterns of sensitivity. Our awareness of any certain change in these cells is received by us in the form of a thought. When something causes the same pattern of cells to be stimulated again, we are conscious of the same thought again. For instance, if we see a dog bite a man, this experience, like all others, causes a certain group of cells to become sensitized, and the sight of a dog at a later time might either reproduce our awareness of this complete cell pattern, which to us would be the thought of the dog biting the man, or it might merely reproduce the awareness of having seen a dog before. In which case, we may ask, will such a situation stimulate the complete pattern (of the dog biting the man), and in which case will it reproduce the impression of a dog only? First, THE CONDITIONS THAT PREVAIL at the time of the first exposure of the pattern of cells (the first sight and impression of the event) exert a great influence upon this probability of recall, as do the TIME PERIODS between later exposures.

When we see another dog, other things being equal, the greater the number of other details which were included in the original scene that we observe in the surrounding panorama of objects and things, the greater will be the certainty of the complete cell pattern being stimulated, with its consequent reproduction of the original scene in various degrees of perfection. The quantity of these associated details necessary to recall is influenced by the recency of the original event to be recalled and the number of the associated stimuli to which we have recently reacted. The quantity of associated stimuli necessary to reproduce the whole impression seems to vary proportionately to the INTENSITY of the original response, which is governed by the conditions under which it was originally attached to the stimulus pattern.

One of these conditions is what psychologists call "Mental Set,"—that is, desire to learn. Mental Set at the time of learning increases the probability of recall in the future. Things can be remembered, however, without desire or "set." An impression is intensified—that is, the cells are made more susceptible and probability of recall is increased—by attention. When the mind is centered upon only one thing or one idea, and all distractions are cut off, the impression is more apt to be recalled the next time even a partial stimulus occurs. This intensification of a response to a stimulus also occurs when considerable emotion, such as anger or fear, accompanies the original stimulus.

In hypnosis the mental set is intensified, the attention is increased and distractions are cut off.

SUGGESTION FOR MEMORY IMPROVEMENT

Because I want (state your reason) I have perfect recall. Everything I hear, see, think or experience is recorded in my mind. My mind is a computer. This information is available to me at any time because it is permanently recorded in my mind. I have a permanent record of names, dates, faces, and all other things I have learned, and I recall them easily. All I have to do is ask my subconscious mind for the information I want by pretending to push the "answer" button. I think the word "answer" and in a few seconds the answer is delivered to my conscious mind. I read pages of material and every bit of it is available to me when I push the answer button. My computer goes to work, and supplies me with the information which I have recorded and retained.

Memories are also staying in my conscious mind longer. I instantly recall things I have studied or experienced more recently. My concentration is perfect, and anything I concentrate on, I retain in my conscious mind. My conscious mind is expanding, and it retains more and more information for instant recall. Memories stay in my conscious mind much longer. If any older memory isn't instantly recalled I send an order to the subconscious computer. It is reliable and foolproof, and it sends me the answer. I just think "answer," and imagine I am pushing the answer button and the answer comes to me. The ideas in this suggestion are symbolized by the word "Computer."

This is an example of a suggestion written in the first person. Change to the third person if you record it.

Everything you have ever experienced is actually recorded in your subconscious mind, so this suggestion is not exaggerated. If you repeat this suggestion daily you will observe an astonishing improvement in your memory.

LEARNING AND SELF HYPNOSIS

Acquiring knowledge is the process of attaching responses to stimuli. Upon seeing a cat, we recognize it if we have seen one before. If we have never seen a cat before, we recognize its similarity to an animal which we have seen, and our new impression is the comparative difference. After learning to read the word "cat," and to attach the three letters to the sight of a cat, we remember the animal when we see the word printed. The printed word serves as a substitute stimulus for the sight of a cat. This is called association learning.

Three types of learning are observable in the human being: trial and error, imitation, and insight. The first, trial and error learning, is merely a process of elimination of unsuccessful or unnecessary actions and an establishment of the successful ones necessary to attain a desired goal. This is the type of learning usually followed by lower animals, although humans use it in the learning of many sports and skills in which muscular coordination is necesary. The second type of learning, imitation, is explained by its title. Imitation accounts for a great many of our actions. The third type, insight learning, is the sudden grasping of a solution to a problem after "thinking it over." This insight is actually a process of "mental trial and error" in which like situations in past experiences are compared with the present problem until a solution is hit upon.

Learning might be called modification of behavior as the result of experience. In its simplest form, learning results from the stimulus response sequence. Repetition of a stimulus with a certain RESPONSE OF THOUGHT renders the connection between the two more certain, provided that attention and observation accompany the practice. Repetition of a stimulus with a type of response that is an act OTHER THAN THINKING OR REMEMBERING will strengthen the THOUGHT CONNECTION between the two. The interpretation (pleasantness or unpleasantness) is responsible for our committing or inhibiting the act. Hypnosis not only heightens the attention and concentration, but it also permits us to change the interpretation!

Repetition is not necessary to learning, for less or even no repetitions need occur if the material to be learned has sufficient meaning to us, or if its presentation is accompanied by intense emotion or interest. The amount of repetitions necessary to learning seems to vary proportionately to the intensity of the motivating factors, the meaningful connection of the material to material previously learned, or a combination of the two.

Hypnotism increases motivation and increases concentration. Following is an example suggestion which will increase your ability to learn.

SUGGESTION FOR PERFECT CONCENTRATION

Because you want to learn more rapidly and with less effort (or choose your own reason) you concentrate more perfectly every day. You know that a person in hypnosis can concentrate upon and learn pages of material, so you narrow your attention down to one thing as though you were in hypnosis. You set a time limit of one hour, and when you are ready to concentrate you say the words "Narrow down." Your attention immediately narrows down to the job you have to do. The noises around you fade into the distance. You are oblivious to your surroundings. There is only one job to do and nothing else exists for you. Only in an emergency will your concentration be broken, and then you are concentrating again the minute you attend it. Your concentration is perfect until the time limit you set arrives. You are oblivious to your surroundings and you think only of the job you set out to accomplish. You narrow down your thoughts to the one thing. Your concentration is perfect and remains that way for the time you set. Your concentration is constant and perfect. Your concentration is perfect! When you say "narrow down" the world seems to fade away except for the job you are concentrating on. You have perfect control. You concentrate and comprehend with ease. You concentrate perfectly.

(If not recorded): These thoughts come into my mind when in hypnosis. They are symbolized by the words "Narrow down."

Remember to be enthusiastic while recording your suggestion and if you symbolize it, read it with exaggerated emphasis. Your conscious mind may think it sounds silly, but you are not trying to impress it. Your subconscious has no critical factor and it believes anything it is told, so the thicker you spread it on, the better the results.

SELF CONFIDENCE

The motivating factor for the following suggestion might be: "Because I want to succeed in life" or "Because I want people to like me."

SUGGESTION FOR INCREASING SELF-CONFIDENCE

Because (insert your reason) you have confidence in yourself. This confidence is growing daily. As you go deeper into hypnosis you see yourself, in your imagination, speaking calmly and confidently to a gathering of people. Their attention is all directed upon you. You are enjoying being the center of attention. The crowd likes you, and you like them. You find it easy to make friends. People like you. You have confidence and poise. You are interested in people and they are interested in you. You listen to what they say with great interest. People like you because you are a good listener. They know they can depend upon you for good advice. You have a great ability to reach decisions, and people know your advice is worth listening to. You have confidence when you go to a party. You mix with people and have fun. You make friends easily because you are genuinely interested in people. Your confidence in yourself grows daily. You like people and you like yourself. You have lots of abilities and talents, and they are becoming more apparent every day. You believe in yourself and you are on your way to success. You can do anything that is necessary for your well-being and happiness, because you have perfect confidence in yourself. You can handle any situation you meet. You have confidence in your ability to meet new people and make new friends. People like you because of your confident personality, your warm, friendly smile and your charming manner. You radiate frienship and good will. Your personality is growing daily. Your confidence is growing daily. You have poise, and you are comfortable, relaxed and at ease on every occasion.

(If not recorded): All of the ideas in this suggestion are symbolized by the word "Self-esteem" (or insert your own symbol).

ACHIEVEMENT OF GOALS

In Chapter One we described the subconscious mind as a goal-striving mechanism. Unless you program it with positive goals it is programmed by chance and circumstance, and is often working to achieve negative goals such as ill health, marital strife, failure or financial loss. You have the ability to change the script, and reprogram it. Once a positive goal of your own choosing is established in it, your subconscious mind uses all of its power and energy to attain that goal. What the subconscious perceives it achieves.

First you must determine what you want out of life. Financial success? A successful career? A complete education? You must have a strong desire to succeed because your subconscious can't be fooled. You don't know very much about your subconscious but it knows everything that is in your conscious mind. It wants to be guided, and if you program it to work toward a goal, and have a strong desire to reach that goal, it will see that you reach it.

There are several things to remember while reprogramming your subconscious to work toward long-range goals.

BE SPECIFIC. Don't say you want financial success. Tell you subconscious what business you want to succeed in.

BE PRACTICAL. Don't say you want to be a heavyweight boxer if you weigh one hundred and eight pounds and have a light bone structure.

You would undoubtedly gain weight and acquire great muscular strength, but the gap is too wide unless you want to set a greatly extended time limit. Be optimistic though, because the seemingly impossible often happens. Many salesman have doubled their lifetime sales record through the use of auto suggestion the month after learning it.

USE YOUR IMAGINATION

Write your affirmation, and before and after you read it aloud several times, close your eyes and create in your conscious mind an image of how you want things to be when you reach your goal. Imagine how you will act, and how you will feel. See a clear mental picture of yourself, and enjoy the daydream. Plato said, "We become what we contemplate." Christ said, "As a man thinketh, so is he." Your subconscious mind understands pictures better than words. Imagine it will happen, hypnotize yourself and tell your subconscious to make it happen, believe it will happen, and it will.

A recording executive who is a friend of mine programmed himself to win a certain golf tournament. He set a deadline of five months for his subconscious to improve his skill enough to win. He won the tournament and brought his prize cup in for us to admire. Then he confided in us that his business had gone downhill to such an extent during the past five months that he was practically broke. He had been so interested in his golf he had neglected to make a living. He realized what he was doing, but he was so interested in winning the tournament that he was willing to make the sacrifice. He promptly reprogrammed his subconscious to succeed in his business, and shortly thereafter produced a best selling record!

I give this example to illustrate the intensity of a subconscious drive. You must choose your goals carefully, and learn to modify them if something else of importance is being neglected. A goal chosen in a frivolous manner can cause you to neglect other more worthwhile goals.

IF YOU WANT TO QUIT SMOKING

If you have a strong desire to quit smoking you can do it by using self-hypnosis. If, however, you are merely wondering about whether self-hypnosis can "stop" you, forget it. And if you are one who exclaims (with a cough) "No one is going to stop me from smoking," make sure you read the formula for relief of pain in chapter six. It will help when you get your cancer or your emphysema!

Smoking is not the glamorous habit it used to be. The old "Hail fellow, well met, let's light up a cigarette" attitude is changing to one of "Is he still sucking on that stinking thing?"

Even since it was proven conclusively that five times as many smokers contracted lung cancer or emphysema, and heart attacks were more prevalent in smokers than in non-smokers, smokers began to look either foolhardy or ignorant of the facts. Millions have quite smoking, and millions more hope to.

While the original non-smoker was resigned to breathing smoke blown out of someone else's lungs, the former smoker who has kicked the habit is more vocal about this abuse. Laws are being passed which ban smoking in public buildings. Department stores are posting no smoking signs to protect the health of their customers and their employees. A great many people are beginning to look at the smoker, not as an admirable he-man or a glamorous woman of sophistication, but as an object of pity.

These are the concepts you can use in your affirmation for the negative side of smoking, along with a healthy fear of death from cancer, heart attack or emphysema. Emphasize the pleasant feeling of clear lungs, vibrant health and long life.

If you have a serious desire to shake the habit and be free, here's how:

First, set a date, and make a commitment to yourself that you will never smoke another cigarette after the date you choose. It is best to give yourself from three to ten days to get used to the idea that you will never smoke again. During this period, tell all of your friends, relatives and co-workers that they will never see you smoking again after the date you set. Let's say the date you have chosen is October first. Tell them "You'll never see me smoking again after October 1st."

Don't just tell them you're going to quit smoking after October 1st. Say these exact words: "You'll never see me smoking again after October 1st." This is not just a matter of burning your bridges. Every time you repeat this statement, you reinforce the idea in your own mind that you mean what you say. You strengthen your resolution to quit.

There is a choice of two methods that may be used during this period before you actually become a non-smoker. Some find one more to their liking and some prefer the other. If you choose the first of the two, you will use the following procedure: Smoke twice the number of cigarettes you usually smoke during every waking hour. If you usually smoke one every half hour, smoke one every 12 or 15 minutes. It is important that you smoke when you don't want to, and it is also important that you finish every cigarette that you light. I recommend that you show this procedure to a qualified doctor and get his approval before starting, because this saturation smoking must be continued until you develop an intense aversion to it. When your chosen date arrives, you are ready for it!

The second method is just as good for those who choose it. The period of time before becoming a non-smoker is spent in practicing being free from tobacco enslavement for short periods of time, by gradually cutting down on the quantity of cigarettes smoked. During this period, drink lots of water and take a long deep breath at least once every five minutes. Most smokers only take a deep breath when they inhale. When they don't smoke, they miss these long deep breaths without realizing what they need. The deep breath of clean air with its badly needed oxygen will give you part of the satisfaction you thought you were receiving from the cigarette.

I suggest that you obtain the Gil Boyne hypnotic tape #114 entitled "You can stop smoking now." This tape may be purchased from Westwood Publishing Co., 312 Riverdale Drive, Glendale, CA 91204. Play both sides of this tape daily until the day you become a non-smoker. On this pre-decided day, you start using the following affirmation, at least twice daily. You may use the symbolized suggestion method described on page 49, or the self-recorded method described on page 27.

After you have listened to a hypnotic induction and become hypnotized, the following series of suggestions will reinforce the pride and the satisfaction you gain from being a non-smoker. Enjoy this tape and the pleasant relaxed feelings it gives you at least twice daily.

"And now, as you go deeper into relaxation, you Thoroughly Enjoy the feeling of **Complete Freedom** you get, from **Knowing** you are a Non-Smoker. You feel so **Proud** of yourself. You have chosen **Life** over **Death. Vibrant Health** over **Sickly Weakness!** You have gratifying new respect for your body. Your greatest and strongest desire is Vibrant Health and Radiant Vitality.

You Know that your lungs and your heart are the primary parts of your body that sustain the health and the energy you require to thoroughly enjoy living. And you Respect and Care for your Lungs and your Heart. You have chosen **Health** over **Sickness! Strength** over **Weakness!** And you are Happy! You are now **Free At Last.** You have broken the chains that bound you. And you are Free. You are now one of the Vast Majority of those people who are **Strong** Enough, and **Intelligent** Enough to be **Non-Smokers.** You have made a **Final Decision,** that you are **Now** and **Forever** a Non-Smoker. A confirmed non-smoker for the rest of your life. And you are **Proud.** You feel **Good** about yourself. Better than you've felt for Years!

You are tremendously proud of yourself. Proud of your ability to Step Up, Out Of That Stinking Hole. Up into the Fresh, Clean Air. You **Thoroughly Enjoy** breathing the **fresh, clean air,** that is the Natural stimulant to your lungs.

This is the change your lungs have been **Gasping** for — that your body has been **Crying Out** for — and that your heart has been **Longing** for. And You've Made It! Your lungs welcome the fresh air that they crave. Your heart Rejoices at getting the undiluted oxygen it needs. And you feel **Wonderful!** Proud of your **Ability** to have conquered an unnatural, destructive habit. Now, just relax even more, and go deeper. (PAUSE)

Long, deep breaths make you feel good. At least once, every half hour, you stop whatever you are doing for just a moment, and take a Long, Deep Breath. You hold it in. Then you let it out, close your eyes, and relax all over. As you exhale, think the words **"Relaxed and Free".** This is a wonderful feeling. Now take another long, deep breath, even deeper than before. Hold it in as long as possible. As you finally let it all out, think those same words, **"Relaxed and Free"**. As you think these words, just let a wave of relaxation go from the top of your head to the tips of your toes. You Feel Good All Over! Now relax even more and go deeper into a pleasant hypnotic sleep. (PAUSE)

Now visualize yourself, and Feel yourself as a healthy, happy Non-Smoker. You are now **Free.** You now move with greater ease and confidence. You feel better than you've felt for years. You are **Proud** of yourself —**Proud** of your ability to conquer Any habit. You are **Strong!** You feel better with each day that passes. Imagine, and Feel your clean healthy lungs. Each breath of fresh air causes you to feel Better and Better. A satisfying sense of **Pride** sweeps over your entire body, and you feel a Wonderful, Exhilarating sense of **Freedom . . . No Longer A Slave.** You are **Free,** and Feeling Great! Enjoy feeling this wonderful, satisfying feeling — Now. (PAUSE)

Now go deeper, and let go even more, and enjoy this pleasant relaxed feeling. Imagine your self, now, walking past a group of several of these miserable people, who are still sucking on their pacifiers, and breathing in their body-poisoning smoke, and blowing it out into the air for others to breathe. You don't Hate them. You don't even Dislike them. You **Understand** them. You understand their Crippling Weakness, so you **Tolerate** Them. Poor Things. They can't help it. They're just **Stuck!** You sympathize with them. Many of these weaklings would like to kick this vicious enslaving habit, but they don't know how. Others of this group may be good hearted, nice people, but too ignorant to understand the chances they are taking. And some are too young to be wise. Some may be so unhappy with the lives they are making for themselves they **Choose** to die, or feeling so guilty, they choose to die in the **Horrible Manner.** They may be punishing their body for something their mind made them do. This is absurd. But You are far Superior to these poor misguided people. You have a Profound Respect for the body you were born in. This is **Your** body, and you treat it with **respect.** And it, in turn, makes you feel healthy and happy, physically, mentally and spritully.

Although you don't like it, you Tolerate the second hand smoke from these poor victims of their habit, because you are sorry for them. They believe that they can't help being weak. They are ignorant of their ability to escape from the rut they are in. Hopefully, many of them will find the way, and join the healthy ranks of the enlightened majority. But, sadly, some will die, years before their time. Of emphysema, lung cancer or heart disease.

We can only pity them, and be kind to them while they last — and tolerate their poison smoke and their stinking breath. Man and womankind has always had to suffer with the weak and the ignorant. This is life, and you generously accept your role. (PAUSE)

You are now, and forever, a **confirmed Non-Smoker.** Your **Final Decision** Is **Made** and **Agreed To,** and every day that passes reinforces it.

Picture, and imagine, in your mind, someone offering you a cigarette. You always answer "No, I've kicked that habit." You say that **Proudly.** "No, I've kicked that habit." You might add, if you feel it necessary, "I don't mind if you have one," but you always add "No, I've kicked that habit."

Every time you refuse an offer of a cigarette, you feel an Invigorating sense of Power and Pride. You are **Proud** of being one of the **vast majority** — the people who have the **Guts** to become, and stay NON-SMOKERS. You are Proud Of The Fact that **you** Have What It Takes, **Guts, Intelligence,** and **Self Respect** — and Common Sense.

You know, that the Longer Your Remain Free of this Repulsive Habit, the easier it is to Remain free of it, because you feel better with every day that passes. Better in Body, Mind and Spirit. You Thoroughly Enjoy this invigorating feeling of Physical Well Being, Mental Health, and Emotional Self Respect.

You feel good all over, and Proud that You, and You Alone, are in charge of your body.

You always enjoy the pleasant, relaxed feeling of self hypnosis, and you have an overwhelming desire to listen to this tape twice every day. You always feel completely rejuvenated and refreshed when you come out of hypnosis, because the complete, restful relaxation causes your body to become completely normalized. Your blood pressure is normal, your glands are working in harmony with one another, your body chemistry is balanced, and you **Feel Good!**

Now, just relax even more, and enjoy a moment of silence, during which all of these true ideas and concepts make a deep and lasting impression upon your subconscious mind, never to be removed. This moment of silence starts right now. (PAUSE)

Then proceed with the usual wake-up procedure, and you will come back to awareness feeling completely refreshed, and proud of your ability to control your own behavior. You are now the boss!

EAT ANYTHING YOU WANT
AND "THROW YOUR WEIGHT AWAY"

The usual method of reducing is diet. Dieting brings about overeating. The weight goes down, but then goes back up. This sequence results in a constant feeling of failure, and each succeeding failure reinforces the belief that the next attempt will fail. Few, if any, will accept the idea of a lifetime of deprivation. Therefore, depriving yourself of the food you want is not the answer, if you want to obtain and maintain a healthy, attractive figure.

Through the use of hypnotism you can attain a healthy, normal weight and maintain it permanently while eating as much as you want. But you won't want any more than your body needs. You eat only when you are physiologically hungry and you enjoy the food more.

You will know the difference between physiological hunger and psychological hunger. To reduce and maintain in this manner, follow the following procedure. First, choose the ideal weight that you believe is right for you. Visualize yourself at this ideal weight. Some people, who have always been overweight, have difficulty doing this because they have never seen themselves thin. If you find it difficult to visualize, find a picture in a magazine of a person with a shape you admire. Cut the picture out, and imagine yourself with that figure. It may take a little practice, but this is important. Keep the picture, and look at it often. **Know** that your body will take that shape, and it will. **What is expected tends to be realized.**

Next, look at yourself in a full length mirror as you are now. Do you like what you see? Now visualize yourself as you want to look and compare! Since hypnotism cannot make you do anything you don't want to do, this will help you decide what you really want.

A small percentage of people have a strong desire to loose weight, but their subconscious desire is to keep it. When the conscious and the subconscious minds are in conflict, the subconscious will always win over a period of time. Your conscious mind is the mind of choice, but your subconscious mind is the mind of preference. You choose what you prefer. If you prefer to do something that is detrimental to your health and happiness your subconscious mind always has some reason (rationalization) to believe this behavior to be necessary. If there is some subconscious reason why you are keeping your excess weight, it must be faced and dealt with, and I will explain how to do this later in this chapter. Fortunately, these cases are the exceptions and if you are the average overweight person you will find the following method an enjoyable and satisfying way to eat less and enjoy it more!

The following positive and beneficial concepts fed into your computer-like subconscious mind during self hypnosis will free you from destructive, self defeating eating habits while allowing you to eat without conscious restriction or depivation. You will eat what you want but you won't want to eat destructively.

1. You eat only when you are physiologically hungry.

2. You eat and want only foods that are good for your body.

3. You always sit down when you eat.

4. You enjoy drinking water. You find it very cool and refreshing, and you like the taste. You find yourself much more thirsty than you formerly were.

5. Your stomach is smaller, and getting smaller with every day that passes.

6. You remember that stuffy feeling you felt after those big Thanksgiving and Christmas dinners. You have that stuffy feeling. You visualize your stomach as small.

7. You always leave food on your plate.

8. You are enjoying a new eating habit. You always lay your eating utensil down between bites, and think only of the bite that is in your mouth. (Most overweight people bolt their food and are thinking of the next bite instead of enjoying the bite that is in their mouth)

9. You are enjoying a new tasting habit. Because you think only of the bite that is in your mouth, you enjoy the taste of it much more. Your taste buds become more sensitive, and you get much greater satisfaction from each bite. You eat more slowly, you eat much less, but you enjoy it more.

10. Sweets are unpleasant to you. They always remind you of a plate of granulated sugar with thick sticky syrup poured over it.

11. Your goal is to get rid of three pounds of this ugly unwanted fat each week. Picture, in your mind, three 16 oz. raw steaks tied around your body. You throw away this much size each week, and your body looks and feels much better.

12. You exercise more. The more you exercise, the better you feel, and the better you feel, the more you exercise.

13. You are looking better and you are feeling better. Your clothes are fitting looser.

14. You feel good about yourself. You find yourself smiling more and walking differently. Everybody is noticing how good you look!

A total of many thousands of pounds have been discarded by happy people who are using the following affirmation daily to gain and maintain the size and shape they desire. They are eating anything they want and as much as they want, but they don't want much! Because the suggestion is quite long, the results are more effective if you use hypnotic tape. Just read the induction method that you respond to best from chapter two of this book. Record it slowly, in a soft voice. Follow it with any deepening techniques you find necessary to attain a state of deep relaxation. Then read the following affirmation into the recorder, emphasizing the words you think necessary. Follow it by the awakening procedure from page 51. AFFIRMATION FOR THROWING YOUR WEIGHT AWAY.

"Now, as you go deeper into pleasant relaxation, you realize that you have a right to enjoy a perfect body, a perfect size and a perfect shape.

This is your own body, and you have a tremendous respect for it. You have now chosen an ideal weight and size for your body, and you constantly visualize this ideal look as the **real you.** You now inform your inner mind of your overwhelming desire to reach and maintain this ideal size and weight.

Now, relax even more, and as you let go, more and more, picture and imagine that you are standing alone in a large, pleasant room. This room is your own secret place — a restful, peaceful place, where you come every day to relax and enjoy being and feeling slim and attractive — to enjoy being the real you with your ideal figure.

Now imagine how your room is furnished. Choose the color of the walls — the color of the rich, soft carpeting. And also notice that the one wall is completely covered with a beautiful spotless mirror. It is reflecting the beauty of you room, and it also reflects you. You were never so happy! You are always your ideal size and weight when you are in this room, and you come here often to relax and feel happy. You **thoroughly enjoy** posing, and admiring yourself in this large lovely mirror. You **admire** your **attractive body.** Just look at yourself from a side view now, and enjoy knowing this beautiful, attractive person is **you.** You are **thrilled** and **happy** with the image you see! You now sit down, in a very comfortable chair, and look at your beautiful figure while seated. You are growing very fond of this restful chair, and as you sink back into its soft surface, you go deeper and deeer in relaxation. You just feel **terrific,** mentally, physically and emotionally. It's a wonderful feeling to be **healthy, slender** and **attractive.** And it's so **easy.** You wonder why you haven't done it before.

You look so good, and you feel so good. And you are good. You do good things for yourself, because you deserve the best life has to offer. The process is going on right now, and you are enjoying a new, positive personality! Looking at yourself, and admiring yourself, and knowing that the reason you look so good, and feel so good is the result of your new respect and love for your body. It is also the result of your new eating habit.

You eat **only** when you are **sitting down.** When mealtime comes you sit down, and you enjoy eating more than you've ever enjoyed it before. You enjoy the **taste** of food more, because of your new **tasting** habit. Your food tastes so much better, because you give your taste buds a chance to savor and enjoy every bite. You take a bite of food into your mouth. You then lay your eating utensil down, or if it is food you hold in your hand, you lay it down.

You think only of the bite that is in your mouth. You concentrate your entire attention upon that **one bite.** You feel the texture of the food. You find that it tastes better in certain parts of your mouth than in others. You **feel** it in your mouth. You find that the **taste** is more important than the food. You concentrate your entire attention upon the bite that you are chewing, and you enjoy every bit of taste it has to offer. Finally, you swallow it. **Only then** do you even consider another bite. Only when you swallow the delicious bite you are chewing do you take another bite into your mouth, and it tastes wonderful also. It tastes **so good** — because you concentrate your entire attention upon this new bite you are chewing. You have learned that single bites taste much better. Only when you have enjoyed the second bite to its fullest, and swallowed it, do you take another bite. You repeat this process, bite after delicious bite, enjoying every bite to its fullest.

Your taste buds thank you, for allowing them to taste and savor each bite the way nature intended them to do. **Your stomach thanks you,** because it remembers that terrible stuffy feeling that it felt after those huge Christmas or Thanksgiving dinners. **Your body thanks you,** for allowing it to become beautiful, healthy and vigorous. And you are **happy!**

Each time you think of food, when your body is in need of nourishment, you sit down, and you eat slowly, and enjoy every bite, using your thrilling new eating habit. Each time you think of eating when your body does **not** need food, you have an enjoyable new way of dealing with this. You hypnotize yourself. And this is so easy! You take a long, deep breath, and hold it in and count to ten slowly. Then you close your eyes, exhale, and think the words **"calm** and **relaxed"**. Those are your key words, and as you exhale and think these key words, **"calm** and **relaxed"**, you allow yourself to relax all over, every muscle, every ligament and every nerve in your body. Let them all go loose and limp. Repeat this procedure and let your mind go to your secret room, if only for a few seconds. Then open your eyes and decide whether you need food now, or whether you wish to enjoy it more, by waiting until you know it will taste much better. Of course, you **do know** that you enjoy food a great deal more later, because the more you save up your hunger, the better the food tastes and the more you enjoy it. Now, go deeper into relaxation, and visualize yourself making the decision you know will give you the most health, happiness, and progress toward your goal of being your ideal size and weight. (PAUSE)

You **always** leave food on your plate. When you leave food on your plate, as you always do, you know that you have a choice. You don't need this food, so it's wasted, no matter where you put it; in your stomach, in a garbage pail, or in the garbage disposal. It is still waste matter. It will harm your body, but it won't harm a garbage pail — or a garbage disposal. And **you** are not a garbage pail, or a garbage disposal. You respect your body, and you eat only what your body needs.

Now just go deeper. And enjoy this pleasant relaxed feeling. (PAUSE)

Just picture in your mind, now, a quarter of a slice of bread. You **always** leave a portion of food, about this size — about the size of a quarter of a slice of bread, or larger, whether it be bread, meat, vegetable, potatoes, or some other food. You have a strong desire to leave a quantity of food on your plate, equal in volume to a quarter of a slice of bread or larger. You eat only when you are physiologically hungry and your body needs food. That is why you enjoy the taste of food more than you have enjoyed it for years. Your inner mind knows the difference between **real** hunger and **fool's** appetite. You've heard of fool's gold. Inexperienced prospectors used to find and collect it, and travel may weary miles back to civilization hoping to sell it, only to be disappointed and frustrated. Foolish appetite is just like fool's gold. When you mistake it for real body need, you are always frustrated and disappointed as a result of eating. Boredom is not hunger. Worry is not hunger. Disappointment is not hunger and Frustration is not hunger. These feelings are **foolish** appetite — and you are certainly not a fool. You are born to be a unique, one of a kind individual, and you are what you were created to be. A beautiful, perfect human being. (PAUSE)

You have a new and powerful method of dealing with the stress factors in your life. If at any time, something displeases you, or bores you, or, if you feel foolish appetite, you rely upon your new habit, of taking a long, deep breath. You hold it in and count to ten. Then you let it all out, and relax all over. Let your eyelids close down, and say these words to yourself, "calm and relaxed." You just feel wonderful. You open your eyes feeling **good.**

You **know** that **foolish appetite** cannot be satisfied with food, because it's not real. Being deceived by **foolish** appetite only punishes your body. Heeding **real** hunger is **natural** and **satisfying.** Because you understand this, you only eat when you are **physiologically** hungry. Only when your body needs food. And your body is showing it!

Go back to your beautiful mirror in your secret room, now, and look at your beautiful body — the **real** you. You love the way you look. And you find yourself merging with this image, more every day, and you are becoming this image. You are much more confident now. Everyone is noticing how good you look. You find yourself smiling, more and more, because you are feeling so good about yourself. You feel so happy, that you are in complete charge of your mind, your body, and your spirit.

And now relax even more, and go deeper while you allow all of these true and beneficial ideas and concepts to make a deep and lasting impression upon your subconscious mind, never to be removed.''

After a pause, read the wake-up procedure into the recorder in an energetic tone of voice. Play this tape to yourself twice every day, and you will find yourself not wanting to eat unless you are physiologically hungry. Your subconscious mind now knows psychological hunger as foolish appetite, which it is. You will find yourself wanting less and less food as you continue to listen to this tape twice daily. And you will be happy!

People vary in their response to hypnosis. Some will find themselves desiring less food after listening to this suggestion for two or three days, and they will find themselves getting rid of their excess weight quite rapidly. They will be amazed at how easy it is, because they find themselves eating less without realizing why. They don't want food that their body doesn't need. Some may find that it takes longer, two weeks, three weeks or even a month. But never give up! If only occasionally you find yourself not wanting to finish a meal, or refusing to eat when you would formerly have done so, these are positive results. Continue to listen to the tape and you will find yourself wanting less and less food. You will enjoy the food you eat more, but you will find yourself wanting less.

WHEN YOU NEED THE HELP OF AN
CERTIFIED HYPNOTHERAPIST*

Without realizing it, some people eat in self defense. Others may be eating to punish themselves, or to punish someone else. They are usually consciously unaware of the reasons for their eating problems, so their subconscious must be reached and influ-

*For referral to Certified Hypnotist/Hypnotherapist write to: The American Council of Hypnotist Examiners, 312 Riverdale Dr., Glendale, CA 91204.

enced before their self-destructive behavior can be changed. Often, some event or series of events, which occured before their conscious minds were developed sufficiently to reject harmful ideas, left them with subconscious belief that an unnatural eating habit was the best way out of some dilemma. This became a part of their subconscious belief system, and it must be faced and dealt with before the eating pattern can be changed. The untrue idea accepted at an earlier age must be substituted with the truth before normalcy can be established.

The Hypnotherapist will often use age regression to discover the reason for your subconscious mind's mistaken belief that a destructive eating habit is necessary to your welfare. While hypnotized, you will remember in great detail the period in your life in which you first started to eat excessively. Then, from an adult viewpoint, you will understand yourself and the reason for your abnormal behavior. This understanding has long been thought by prominent therapists to be sufficient to change behavior, but in many cases the results have fallen far short of expectations. The Hypnotherapist will convince your subconscious mind that your present eating habit was chosen without sufficient knowledge at the time, or that the purpose it served originally is now outdated, or that, if the problem still exists, you can find a more satisfactory way of handling it.

This will free you from your subconscious drive to eat the excess. The two levels of your mind will agree that you, as a total person, will be happier with normal eating habits and normal weight and health will result.

One of my clients, while hypnotized, remembered the doctor's conversation with their mother when she was less than a year old. He had said, "That child has to eat or she'll die." Her mother probably reinforced the idea of death from not eating numerous times while the child was convalescing, and a subconscious opinion that eating was escaping death was formed. Although she didn't know it consciously, she was driven to eat excessively to feel safe. Some women have strong sexual desires but have been programmed to believe these feelings are wrong or sinful. One of my clients, who weighed almost three hundred pounds, had a subconscious desire to be unattractive to men, and thus avoid temptation, yet she was not consciously unaware of the reason for her over eating. Since she was now happily married, the original need for this self destructive habit had long since disappeared, but her subconscious mind had to be informed of this fact before it would stop driving her to do what her conscious mind knew was killing her.

Fortunately, deep rooted subconscious problems that force people to eat destructively are the exception rather than the rule. People adopt unhealthy eating habits for many reasons, including boredom, and emotional upset. Sometimes eating acts as a substitute for love. "Nobody loves me enough, so I'll be good to myself," so they give themselves a treat. Many are programmed during early childhood to associate food with health. They are bombarded with phrases such as, "You want to grow up to be strong and healthy, don't you?" Or, "One more bite — it's good for you," or "You need this for energy." The list goes on and on. Some men equate size with power. They found out at an early age that they could push smaller boys around and get their own way. As adults they know consciously that fat is a poor substitute for muscle, but their subconscious still drives them to eat more in a constant effort to increase their size.

Suggestions to children such as, "If you are good I'll give you some candy," or, "Clean up your plate so you can have dessert," offer a reward for eating, and pride is appealed to by such suggestions as "He has a marvelous appetite!," or "He eats like a horse! A healthy appetite."

Is it any wonder the American public is eating itself to death while many in other nations are starving? Most people in our country do not eat because they are hungry. They eat because they are programmed to eat, and they can be **re-programmed,** and self-hypnosis is the best and most effective method of reprogramming!

PHYSIOLOGICAL BASIS OF THE
SUBCONSCIOUS MIND

There has been some argument among psychologists about the location of the subconscious mind. From the viewpoint of brain surgeons this argument can be settled with certainty and clarity.

We cannot see a mind, conscious or subconscious. Neither can we see heat or cold. But we can trace any of these to its source and establish its existence by its interaction with other entities.

The mind is the result of brain activity, and without the brain there would be no mind as far as human functioning is concerned. This fact has been proved conclusively by observing the results of injuries or lesions in various areas of the brain. By this method we have also established the location of the areas that function at a level of awareness, and those which function involuntarily, or at a subconscious level.

The conscious mind is identified with the somnic nervous system which innervates the voluntary muscles, the controlling force of which lies in the cerebral cortex, the outer coating of the brain. The area that receives information from the senses is located in a lateral strip across the top of the head at the front portion of the Parital lobe of the cerebral cortex, and the area that controls voluntary movements is located just in front of it, at the back of the frontal lobe. The thinking, reasoning area is located in the extreme frontal area. The first awareness of crude sensations is registered in the thalamus, located at the base of the cerebrum. Its interaction with the sensation receiving area of the cortex adjusts the intensity of feeling, and if it were not for the nerve connections between these two areas, intense suffering would result from a pin prick, and the pressure of clothing would be unbearable. The Thalamus and portions of the Cerebral Cortex, then, are the locations of the physical components of the conscious mind.

The subconscious mind is identified with the autonomic nervous system. It is the activity of those areas of the brain that control and regulate the involuntary or smooth muscles, such as those of the heart, the lungs, the digestive system and the glands. It is also associated with the areas in which memories are stored. The autonomic nervous system is sometimes called the vegetative nervous system because minimal, if any, direct conscious control is possible except through hypnosis.

Only recently it was discovered that memories were stored in the temporal lobe of the cerebral cortex, located near the temple. A surgeon can release memories by stimulating tiny nerve cells, of which there are billions in the human brain. This stimulation activates cell patterns which have been previously sensitized to retain impressions, and for each tiny spot stimulated the memory of a different experience or event is recalled in the minutest detail. These are often long forgotten or deeply buried memories. When the stimulation is removed the memory ends. When the stimulation is reapplied, the memory is recalled again, not where it left off, but from the beginning, just as mechanically as the replaying of a phonograph record. This certainly adds weight to the theory that every impression from our senses is retained by chemical changes in groups of brain cells, and under proper conditions or stimulation these impressions may be brought back to conscious awareness.

The cerebellum, situated in the back of the brain stem, is the storehouse for chain motor responses which are learned by trial and error as we mature. It operates below the level of consciousness, coordinating and blending the movements of the voluntary muscles. The frontal lobe of the cortex, or conscious mind, directs these movements, and the cerebelum gives detailed instructions to the muscles enabling them to operate efficiently. When the cerebellum is injured the motions become jerky and uncoordinated. The cerebellum, then, is also a part of the subconscious mechanism.

The hypothalamus, buried deep in the brain, is the director of much of our subconscious activity, because emotion triggers its action. It is the integrating center for the autonomic nervous system. It controls the body temperature, water retention, and blood sugar by regulation of glandular secretion in the blood. It directs the body's rhythms and energy, activity and rest, appetite and digestion, sexual desire and menstrual cycles. If its normal activities are interrupted by abnormal or prolonged emotional disturbance, it causes severe disruption in the bodily functions which results in mental or physical illness or both. The hypothalamus then, directs more of our subconscious activity than any other area of the brain. The principal components of the subconscious mind, then, are located in the hypothalamus, and in portions of the cerebellum and the temporal lobe of the cereberal cortex.

These areas of the human brain in which the conscious and the subconscious mind operate have been well established and mapped, and these facts can be verified by consulting any recent medical or psychiatric dictionary. It has also been firmly established that the subconscious areas can be controlled by hypnosis while the conscious areas are dormant. This should end any controversy among informed, thinking people about the existence and the whereabouts of the subconscious mind, and clarify the role of hypnosis in reaching and reprogramming it.

The central nervous system controls and coordinates and relates the individual to his environment.
GIL BOYNE

CONCLUSION

Average readers do not get this far into a technical book unless they have a more than avid interest in the subject. At this point, I want to compliment both you and myself; you, because you are still reading, and myself because I resisted the temptation to sound profound to impress other writers. If I have been guilty of oversimplification there are other good books available that are more detailed on specific subjects, such as Dave Elman's "Hypnotherapy," Ormand McGill's "Hypnotism and Meditation" and also his "Professional Stage Hypnotism" to name only a few. These interesting books and many more are obtainable from Westwood Publishing Co. of Glendale, California.

I thoroughly enjoyed writing this book because I believed that a clearly written explanation of self-hypnosis was needed. However my greatest enjoyment has come several years after its publication. People have walked up to me on the street and said, "You're the man who changed my life!" Others have written me letters of congratulations. Best of all, is the fact that the sales have snowballed! One person reads the book, and orders two or three more for his friends or relatives. This means that the book has helped him to help himself, and prompted him to want to help others. The fact that I have succeeded in helping many thousands of people to live happier lives far outweighs the monetary gains I have enjoyed. Being an Hypnotherapist is truly rewarding because it is a people-helping profession. I learned everything I know from Gil Boyne, the "Hypnotist of the Stars", who I believe to be the best therapist in the world. I say this because I have been first hand witness to many of his extraordinary successes and cures!

I spent over seven years watching his therapies and observing the results. Newspapers around the world have written of his amazing cures! Dissolving kidney stones! Curing amnesia! Motivating actors and actresses to become stars! The list goes on and on.

Three years ago I left my Brentwood California Clinic and moved to Seattle, Washington. My wife, Joyce, had lived for a number of years in the great Northwest and had a yearning to return. I saw the move as an opportunity to start a training school for professional hypotherapists and to teach just as Gil Boyne taught me! I am now the director of the largest and most successful hypnotism institute in the Pacific Northwest. My students have included police personnel, FBI agents, medical doctors, psychologists, registered nurses, counselors and even retirees who wish to use hypnotism as a part-time avocation to help others. At the age of 77 years I am a slender, healthy non-smoker, and I am busy teaching and demonstrating hypnosis to full classes five nights a week. I feel good about myself because I am teaching others to help others. I am happy and fulfilled and I'm betting I make it to one hundred years — or more!

If you enjoyed my book I'd be happy to hear about it. Write me in care of the publisher.

Charles Tebbetts

PLEASE TURN PAGE FOR CATALOG OF SELF-HELP AND MIND POWER BOOKS AND CASSETTES.

Best Seller!
THE LEARNING BLOCK

By Dean E. Grass

This book introduces a new technique of teaching through mind conditioning that works. It shows the teacher how to make his efforts with his students more successful; it teaches the student how to think and study more effectively; it brings to the parent the much-needed understanding of what makes a slow learner (the learning block) and what can be done to overcome this handicap.

The author has tested his methods in the classroom for over thirty years and has come to the conclusion that the mind acts as a computer that responds to both negative and positive conditioning. He brings out the fact that classroom instruction is a form of hypnosis and good or bad results may be obtained, depending on the teacher. Thus the teacher will learn in this book how to apply the new technique of positive conditioning which makes the student happier and more willing to learn, by the kind of positive mind conditioning that unlocks "the learning block."

What educators say about *The Learning Block:*

Richard E. Hammerle, *Past Principal – Christopher Columbus Junior High School, Canoga Park, California*

"As educators, we are constantly looking for new ways to work with children. Mr. Grass has been interested in mind conditioning for many years . . . his research has been very interesting and positive, and it opens the doors for others to continue research in the same areas."

Robert P. Malcolm, *Principal – Christopher Columbus Junior High School, Canoga Park, California*

"The philosophy that is developed in regard to programming the mind is something that all of us in education should become aware of . . . I feel that this should be a handbook for all new teachers and a guide for those of us who have been in the profession a long time."

Dr. Ewing A. Konold, *Professor of Education – San Fernando Valley State College, Northridge, California*

"*The Learning Block* should open the doors to many phases of research. Techniques and details should be explored in many areas of mind conditioning . . . . Educators have overlooked this phase of mental development long enough."

Softbound – $6.95

HYPNOSIS:
New Tool in Nursing Practice

Edited by Gil Boyne

GIL BOYNE

In this first-of-its-kind textbook, I have collected the writings of a number of registered nurses who have used hypnotism in a great variety of special situations in medical settings. Among more than four thousand persons I have trained in hypnotherapy, there has been an increasing number of nurses who seem to intuitively grasp the central realization that hypnotism is the original and most effective "placebo effect."

The registered nurse is a "natural" hypnotist with a special capacity to use hypnotism creatively with hospital patients. It is the nurse who provides comfort and reassurance, administers pain-deadening medications and allays the patient's anxieties. There are at least three major reasons why the nurse is ideally suited to use hypnosis in patient care.

1. The patient's on-going, primary contact is with the nurse. Physician-patient contact is usually brief in duration and content.

2. Hospitalized patients often develop powerful feelings of helplessness and dependency which can trigger regression to a childlike ego-state. When this happens, the authority of the nurse is greatly magnified and the patient becomes highly responsive to suggestion, direction and instruction.

3. Because most nurses are female, they are often perceived by the patient as a mother surrogate, since it was mother who tended their needs and cared for them when they were sick as children.

The writers in this anthology have bypassed the technical writings of theoretic and experimental investigations, and have devoted themselves to addressing patients' problems with pragmatic methods based on therapeutic response.

The rapid changes in medical practice, the tremendous escalation of hospital costs, and the heavy demand on the physician's time have brought us to the realization that nurses must be given greater responsibility in the therapeutic treatment process rather than being restricted to the role of dispensers of comfort and medicine. It is my conviction that nurses are about to assume a new dimension in health care, gaining recognition as vital forces in the healing process.

Hardbound — 197 pages — $20.00

Best Seller!
HYPNOTISM
& MEDITATION

By Ormond McGill
Certified Hypnotherapist and Author of:
Professional Stage Hypnotism, The Hypnotism and Mysticism of India, How to Produce Miracles, etc.

Interest in both hypnotism and meditation is sweeping the world, but this is the first book that has ever been written that combines the two in a single process. They can be dovetailed into one. In *hypnomeditation,* self-hypnosis and meditation are skillfully blended, and the resulting techniques may be easily applied by persons in all walks of life to meet life with a new awareness and joyousness.

Hypnotism and Meditation is the operational manual for hypnomeditation. It opens new vistas for the hypnotist. Every process is clearly explained so you can put these techniques to work with both yourself and your subjects. **Detailed hypnomeditation formulas are given.** The results of the processes presented in this book are revolutionary. **Fifteen days with hypnomeditation will transform your life.**

Contents in fourteen comprehensive chapters cover: Understanding Hypnosis and Self-Hypnosis; The Power of Suggestion; The Hypnotic State of Mind; Preparing For Successful Conscious Self-Hypnosis; The Technique of Conscious Self-Hypnosis; Self-Hypnosis and Hypnomeditation; Understanding Meditation; Creating Your Inner Space; Techniques of Meditation; The Practice of Hypnomeditation; The White Light of Protection; The Source of Cosmic Power; Preparing for Hypnomeditation; Fifteen Days to Enlightenment; How To Effectively Use This Manual.

Softbound — INTRODUCTORY PRICE — $4.95

Best Seller!
HYPNOTISM AND MYSTICISM OF INDIA

By Ormond McGill
Dean of American Hypnotists;
author of *"Professional Stage Hypnotism."*

Now you can learn ***ORIENTAL HYPNOTISM*** as performed by the Masters of India; there are their secret teachings. Noted author and hypnotist Ormond McGill reveals how the real mysticism and magic of India is accomplished. You are taught how to be adept.

The original draft of this book was written in Calcutta in collaboration with the great Hindu Sage, Sadhu Parimal Bandu . . . it may well be called the "textbook" of the Hindu Hypnotists and Magicians, and reveals secrets that have been closely guarded for centuries and known only to the limited view. Now **these secrets can be yours.** Note the remarkable Table of Contents of subjects covered in depth so you can now perform the mysticism and magic of India:

Hindu Fakir Magic, Genuine East Indian Magic, Oriental Rhythmic Breathing Techniques, The Mastery of the Mind, The Power of Concentration, Oriental Visualization and Projection, The Magic Power of Words and Sound, Learning the Art of Maya, Occidental/Oriental Hypnotism, Silent Psychic Influence, Yogi Mental Broadcasting, The Psychic Control of Events, The Secrets of Yoga Cosmology, Becoming a Master Magician and Hypnotist, Yogi Self-Development.

You are instructed exactly as the Hindu magicians and hypnotists themselves are instructed, showing you exactly how to develop these remarkable powers. Included are detailed instructions in Oriental Hypnotism which is the finest method of hypnotizing ever developed — combining both Oriental and Occidental techniques. You are shown the Yogi Art of Maya for hypnotically controlling the minds of others. How to Read the Akashic Records, Astral Projection, the Yoga Method of Self-Hypnosis that can make a man over completely.

Limited First Edition — Ddeluxe and hardbound, with dust jacket — 208 pages — fully illustrated — $12.50